MU
N

Mike Mulloy

ARROW

Published in the United Kingdom in 2001 by Arrow Books

1 3 5 7 9 10 8 6 4 2

First published in the United Kingdom in 2001 by
Arrow Books

Arrow Books
The Random House Group Limited
20 Vauxhall Bridge Road, London SW1V 2SA

Random House Australia (Pty) Limited
20 Alfred Street, Milsons Point, Sydney,
New South Wales 2061, Australia

Random House New Zealand Limited
18 Poland Road, Glenfield, Auckland 10, New Zealand

Random House (Pty) Limited
Endulini, 5a Jubilee Road, Parktown 2193, South Africa

The Random House Group Limited Reg. No. 954009

www.randomhouse.co.uk

A CIP record for this book is available from the British Library

Papers used by Random House are natural,
recyclable products made from wood grown in sustainable forests.
The manufacturing processes conform to the environmental
regulations of the country of origin

Typeset in Baskerville by MATS, Southend-on-Sea, Essex

Printed and bound in Great Britain by
Bookmarque Ltd, Croydon, Surrey

ISBN 0 09 941599 2

To Carol with my love, and to the memory of her parents, Bill and Elsie Casey

Acknowledgements

There are a great number of people who have assisted, directly and indirectly, in compiling the material for this book. Some have done so unwittingly, not knowing that their contribution would one day appear in print. It is impossible for me to thank them all personally and I must restrict my acknowledgements to those without whose assistance my story may have forever remained an oral one.

Both Tom Hall and Mike Johnson have provided me with companionship and loyalty over a number of years. They have been accessible to me at all times when an incident has been difficult to recall and they have obliged me with the benefit of their own recollections. They figure prominently throughout the pages that follow. This is also their story. I am also indebted to Liverpool City CID. Their officers were a special breed of men and women, dedicated to the service and prepared to make many sacrifices 'to get the job done'. I am proud to have been associated with them.

I am grateful to my sister Imelda who has always been there for me, and to my niece Amanda for our beautiful goddaughter, Cordelia Jane. Finally, thanks are also due to Andy McKillop and Jo Tapsell, from my publishers, for their belief and encouragement.

Foreword

During the late evening of Saturday, 19th March 1949, a lone gunman entered the office of the Cameo Cinema in Webster Road in the Wavertree district of Liverpool. Checking the evening's receipts were the manager and his assistant. Before the intruder had left he had blasted their lives away. His total haul was just over £50. On this fateful night a popular film was being screened entitled *Bond Street*. Incredibly, it featured a double murder.

In a tough but small inner-city area these killings earned the district notoriety and it became known as Murder Mile. As the years went by, the named passed down through the generations as more murders were committed here than in any other part of Liverpool.

In this book, all the events that I have described actually took place. However, the names of those arrested, interviewed or involved in any inquiry have been changed. They are fictional and any resemblance to any person either living or dead is purely co-incidental.

Prologue

The Wavertree area of Liverpool was a close-knit, working-class community on the fringes of the city centre. The narrow streets of terraced houses had stood for generations. In the February of 1975 it looked very much as it had before the war: well populated, with an abundance of corner shops, and an absence of parks and play facilities forcing young children to play in the streets, close to their homes.

Margaret was one of them. A seven-year-old twin, she was the youngest of nine children raised in Garrick Street off Smithdown Road, and well known to her neighbours. Although shy, she was a popular girl, always willing to run errands for the elderly and help anyone. Everybody had a smile for Margaret, as she did for them. She was often described as being like a 'little doll'.

Late one dark Wednesday afternoon, she was playing outside her front door, wrapped up against the weather in a bright pink raincoat. As the day grew colder, one of her friends asked her into her house to play. She was seen leaving there about 4.30 p.m., but never arrived at her home for teatime.

This was so unusual that her mother immediately

became anxious and, with other family members, began to search the vicinity for her. Margaret's aunt went to the neighbour's home where she had been playing. Her friend's 25-year-old brother, Ernie, opened the door. He said he had sent Margaret on a message to the corner shop and was still waiting for her to return.

The aunt went straight to the shop but Margaret had not been seen.

While friends and neighbours scoured the nearby streets and back entries, Margaret's parents wasted no time in going straight to the police station on Lawrence Road, less than a quarter of a mile away. Several officers were immediately added to the search party and, as time passed and anxiety rose, further officers were drafted in. Applying strict search procedures, the officer-in-charge utilised the growing number of neighbourhood volunteers and no stone was left unturned. But nobody could find Margaret.

At eleven o'clock, the officers involved in the search were due to go off duty but instead they carried on, in their own time, without pay. The new shift added to their numbers.

There were a large number of derelict houses in the vicinity and it was thought that Margaret may have decided to go inside one of them and had hurt herself. Though it would have been out of character, no assumptions were made and each house was systematically searched.

Constable Noel Kelly was checking Webb Street, six streets and little more than 200 yards from where Margaret lived. He was knocking on doors and talking to anybody he came across. Number fifty-eight was

4

derelict and the officer pushed the battered rear door open and shone his torch into the deserted kitchen.

'Margaret?' he called out. There was no answer. Slowly, he picked his way through the rubbish that had accumulated behind the door and made his way into the front room. After searching the ground floor, Noel made his way carefully up the stairs. Nearing the top, he saw a small bundle in the shadows of the landing and lifted his torch.

He froze.

Caught in the beam of light was the little face of a young girl. He had found Margaret.

Every parent's nightmare had come true.

Chapter One

I was raised in a council house with my older sister, Imelda, on the working-class Mount Estate in Birkenhead, within walking distance of Prenton Park, home of Tranmere Rovers Football Club. My only other sibling, an elder brother, Terrance Anthony, died in infancy when only a few weeks old.

My father, Tom, Birkenhead born and bred and a devout Catholic, was a time-served painter. Of medium height but sturdy build, he was a quiet, introverted man by nature but also proud and he fought for his rights. Employed at the shipbuilders Cammell Lairds, he was for many years a well-respected shop steward. When war broke out he worked on a number of warships and submarines, including the ill-fated SS *Thetis*, sunk in Cardigan Bay. His job was deemed a reserved occupation and he was unable to enlist. Instead, he became a special constable and worked on the streets of the town throughout the Blitz, spending endless hours through the night looking for people who had been bombed in their homes.

During the Blitz my mother would never seek the sanctuary of the air-raid shelters. She preferred to stay at home in Hilbre Street so that, if anything happened to my father, the police would be able to find her. One night no enemy action was expected and my dad's sergeant allowed him to sign off early to look after my mum. He was no sooner home than the sirens started and he insisted my mum and Imelda went to the shelter. It was possibly the only occasion during the entire Blitz that he was home during an air-raid. When the all-clear sounded, they returned to find our house had been completely obliterated by a German bomb. Had it happened on any other night, my mother and sister would have been killed and I would never have been born.

My mother was a small, outgoing woman, barely five feet tall, who wore her heart on her sleeve, smothering both Imelda and myself with love and attention. She was responsible for discipline in our house but would scold us one moment and laugh with us the next. She was an auxiliary nurse at St Catherine's Hospital on Church Road and later at the cancer hospital at Clatterbridge.

My schooldays were spent at St Anselm's Grammar on Manor Hill, across the road from Birkenhead Park on the edge of the town centre. By the time I left I already knew what I wanted to do with my life. My father had known long periods of unemployment and was keen for me to find an occupation not subject to capital depression. Having served as a special, he fully supported my ambition to go one better and become a fully qualified police officer.

In the January of 1960, at the age of seventeen, I crossed the river and joined the Liverpool City Police as a cadet and was posted to Rose Hill station, close to

Liverpool's famous Scotland Road area. There I was initiated in the more unsavoury aspects of police work, including seeing a dead body for the first time.

With a constable, I had been called to a house in one of the terraced streets off Great Homer Street. The old woman who lived there had not been seen for a few days and, when we forced an entry, we were startled by half a dozen cats rushing past us out of the house. Sadly, we found the old woman dead and a gruesome scene met our eyes. Although she had lain in her bed for just a few days, the starving animals had begun to eat away at the corpse.

Eighteen months later on 14th July 1961, I was sworn in as Constable 188 'F' and posted to Garston Police Station, some six miles south of Liverpool City centre and a mile from Speke airport. Fresh from Bruche Police Training Centre in Padgate, near Warrington, I was met by the man who would introduce me to the realities of becoming a police officer: Sergeant Gill Morris. Like most men of his service in those days, he had war ribbons on his tunic. He had been recruited in an age when all constables had to be at least six feet tall and I can still remember his words to me, spoken in a thick, Scouse accent, as I approached him for the first time.

'Forget everything they told you at Bruche, son. Listen to me and I'll teach you what real policing is all about.'

So that was what I did.

I was only a few short weeks into my service when I was confronted by a suspicious death for the first time. I was on the morning shift on Christmas Day, 1961, and just before ten I was making my way to the station for my meal break. As I walked up St Mary's Road I passed an old woman clad entirely in black. Although they have now practically vanished, these women were a common sight on the streets of Liverpool in those early days and were colloquially referred to as 'Mary Ellens'.

'Mornin' lad. Happy Christmas,' she greeted me.

'Morning love, best of the season to you.'

'How old are you, lad?' she queried.

'Nineteen, why do you ask?'

'Oh lad, you don't look old enough to be out without yer mam!'

That did nothing to help my confidence, neither did the events that followed. Little sense had been made of the hysterical ranting of a woman who had telephoned the emergency services early on that Christmas morning, but the control operator had succeeded in obtaining her address in Speke Road Gardens and I was sent alone to investigate.

The address was a flat in a tenement block and, reaching the top of the internal staircase, I was met by a highly agitated woman on the communal landing.

'Oh, God! Oh, my God! He's dead! Oh, God!'

'It's all right, love. Calm down. What's happened?'

I could get no sense from her but, from one of a number of people gathered around her front door, I gleaned that the woman, having got out of bed, had entered her kitchen and found the battered body of her husband lying on the floor.

Bracing myself, I entered the flat and made for the kitchen. There he was. His head injuries were quite horrific and even the most cursory examination by a

9

teenage bobby was sufficient to establish that the man had been dead for several hours.

I was totally out of my depth and much relieved when the cavalry arrived in the form of senior CID officers. Within hours, the cause of his death was determined, the details of the incident had been discovered and a man had been arrested. Following midnight mass there had been a fracas and the deceased had struck his head on a gravestone. A trail of blood from the scene to the flat revealed that he had managed to stagger home before collapsing.

I was impressed by the professional manner in which the detectives dealt with the incident. That event decided my future: I was determined to become a detective.

Later in the day, I was ordered to attend the post-mortem at the city mortuary close to the old Royal Hospital on Pembroke Place and identify the body to the pathologist. I was also required to remain for the duration of the examination and still recall with a shudder a detective chief superintendent who, interrupted during his Christmas dinner, offered me a turkey sandwich. Nothing on earth could have induced me to accept the invitation and I politely declined. The officer turned out to be the legendary Bert Balmer, who had investigated many notorious murders, including the Cameo Cinema shootings.

The post-mortem revealed that the deceased had an abnormally thin skull. As a result, only a charge of assault occasioning actual bodily harm was eventually brought.

By the time I was released by the pathologist, I had

worked several hours past the end of my shift, but that was considered part of the job. No overtime would be added to my princely wages of £9. 8s. 6d (£9.42) a week.

Chapter Two

I was in uniform for just three years, unusual in those days, and walked the beats of Murder Mile before I was attached to a specialist undercover unit called the Commando Squad. Drastic measures were required to combat the disturbing increase in serious crime in and around the city centre and the unit's unique operation was the first of its kind to be instigated by the police service. For the first time television cameras were used for surveillance and the unit's methods were eventually imitated by many other forces, both in this country and abroad. Within three months the efforts of the Commando Squad led to an incredible 50 per cent reduction in serious crime. It did not come without a cost. Several of my colleagues were seriously injured, one so badly he was no longer able to continue in the service. It was a dangerous game, played out in the back alleys and side streets of the city. During my year-long attachment, well in excess of 1,000 criminals were arrested as a direct result of our endeavours. This led to my appointment as a detective constable in 1965. From now on, I would be known both inside the service and in the criminal world as a 'Jack' – the name (as opposed to a 'knave') that Liverpool detectives were always called.

I was posted to the south end of the city and based at Speke. Within the first week I was called to Essex Street station in Toxteth, on the southern edge of the city centre, in the early hours of a cold and miserable morning. Detective Sergeant Harry Beadle had been tipped off that a 23-year-old woman had been strangled by her common-law husband and her body dumped in a flat in Hatherly Street, close to Upper Parliament Street. The informant had also told him the killer was out on the streets, looking to borrow a car to dispose of the body.

We forced entry into the first-floor flat in a Victorian house, a poky, depressing place, and found a woman's body on the bed. Detectives were allocated different vantage points from where they would await the murderer's return and I was instructed to stay with the corpse.

Alone with this poor dead woman, I felt decidedly uneasy. In the dim light, I lost count of the number of times I thought she moved and could have sworn I heard her breathing. When her killer finally returned and was arrested in the hallway, I was mightily relieved to step out into the cool, early morning air.

My regular partners by then were Mike Johnson and Tom Hall. Mike, a tall, broad ex-seaman, was excellent company even in times of adversity. He had a terrific, dry sense of humour and was a compulsive practical joker. First and foremost though, he was a damn good thief-taker. Like most detectives, the criminal fraternity we dealt with gave him a nickname. Usually they were derogatory but Mike was known simply as the Bear. In my case, my prematurely greying hair which began at

13

the age of twenty-three, and (I like to tell myself) my ingenious style of policing, earned me the nickname of the Silver Fox.

We were fortunate to be shown what the job was all about by a detective sergeant whose name is a legend in police circles: Tom Hall. Tom was a burly man with a heart of gold and limitless humour and compassion. Well read and educated, he has the shrewdest detective mind it has been my pleasure to encounter.

Tom was never given a nickname. He was known to hardened criminals and honest members of the public alike as Mr Hall. Even the villains had respect for Tom.

Working in partnership in the CID is so unique that you are never officially posted with a partner – you select each other. So many hours are spent in each other's company it is vital you get on well. That is not to say that at times you will not have blazing rows. You must also have the same appetite for work and the ability to tune into each other's way of thinking, especially in interviews.

Having acquired the tools of my trade at the sharp end, I was promoted in 1969 to detective sergeant. This meant that, having spent the previous four years as a 'leg man', I would now be called upon more frequently to take part in prime investigations into serious crimes.

Like many others, I had chosen to be a career detective, but God knows why. The hours we worked were ridiculous and taking a day off was a luxury. Regardless of the hours we put in, we were only ever paid our basic salary and a paltry detective allowance. Promotion was far more difficult to attain that it was for uniformed officers. There were many more of them and consequently far more vacancies arose in their department than in ours.

Detective work is for the dedicated. We may have chosen it, but our wives most certainly have not. It takes a certain kind of woman who can tolerate never knowing where her husband is or when he will next be home.

In principle, we were supposed to work a 'day' duty or a 'late' duty, rotating daily. Both duties began at the same time in the morning, but a 'day' duty was supposed to last about ten hours and a 'late' duty fifteen. We were also expected to turn in on three weekends out of four.

In practice, you might be asked to work all the hours God sent. Attached to a major investigation, such as a murder inquiry, home life went completely out of the window. It was a lot to ask a young woman to put up with. On the day my wife Carol and I moved into our new house shortly after we were married, I was out working until three in the morning. It was the first of the countless occasions Carol went to bed alone in that house.

The marked rise in crime in the city during the late sixties was referred to in the local press as 'a wave of terror'. On the streets, the day of the gunman had arrived and armed robberies were becoming wide-spread. They were known as 'blags' and statistics revealed that in Liverpool their occurrence was two and a half times the national average.

By this time, Mike and I were both trained as authorised firearm officers and on numerous occasions we were armed when working. Both Carol and Mike's wife, Sylvia, knew this and it could only have added to their concerns when we were out late.

We would regularly accompany detectives when executing warrants on those suspected of taking part in armed crime. Unfortunately, not everyone was as concerned as Carol and Sylvia about our safety. On one occasion, Tom Hall had gone with other detectives to the city centre Cabaret club in Duke Street to arrest a man wanted in connection with a serious crime. A ruthless gang of thugs attacked them and the officers were badly beaten. They were all hospitalised, one having survived an attempt to bite off one of his testicles. No arrests were made.

Late one Saturday evening a few weeks later, Detective Inspector John Reddington received information that one of the prime instigators of the assault, Sean Walsh, had been seen entering the Blue Angel club in nearby Seel Street. We were warned that he was usually armed and had made it known he would use the gun if ever the police cornered him. From what we knew of him, we had no reason to doubt it. John had also been told he kept a sawn-off shotgun in the boot of his car.

Just after midnight, I was called into headquarters to assist in his arrest. Tom and I were the only authorised firearm officers present. After the briefing we went to draw our firearms, which were only ever issued by a uniformed inspector. We signed for our weapons but, instead of being handed a clip of ammunition each, the Inspector passed us both a single bullet.

Tom looked at him inquisitively. 'What's this?' he asked.

'A bullet,' the Inspector replied, sarcastically. 'It should look familiar.'

'Well, yes, it does,' Tom said. 'But I want a full clip.'

'Why?'

'If I'm forced to fire, my first shot might miss.'

'Bloody jacks!' the Inspector cursed. 'You'd better not miss then, had you?'

I couldn't believe my ears. While we were going to face an armed bloody lunatic, he would be safely shuffling papers and drinking tea behind his desk.

Tom, however, would not be deflected. 'No, boss, you're the one who'd better not miss.'

'What the hell does that mean?' the Inspector roared at him.

'Because if I don't get a full clip,' Tom shouted back, 'you're the one who's going out there with a single bloody bullet and I'm staying here!'

We got the clips.

The next hour seemed to last for ever. The club was heaving with revellers when we got there and the possibility that our target might start firing with so many people about was uppermost in our minds. We kept a low profile and, having identified Walsh, decided we would wait until the club was closing before we confronted him.

Fortunately, he was in no hurry to leave when the club began emptying out and, grasping our opportunity, we made our move. He must have been given some warning because, as we approached him, he bounded across the floor of the club and crashed through the rear fire doors. As we pursued him one of the doormen tried to block our path, which was his mistake. Tom shoulder-charged him and, cannoning backwards, he smashed into the sprinkler system. A torrent of water cascaded down with an immediate devastating effect on the bouffant hairstyles of the female patrons. As we forced our way through the throng nobody even seemed aware of our drawn guns, judging by one girl's comment, 'Where's the bloody rain coming from!'

Walsh scrambled over a wall and dropped to the ground . . . straight into the arms of waiting police officers. A violent struggle ensued but he was eventually overcome without a shot being fired.

We returned to headquarters and went to deposit our firearms.

'Let's have a bit of fun,' Tom said to me quietly. He unloaded the gun and then handed it and the ammunition to the Inspector.

'There's a bullet missing!' the Inspector exclaimed.

'Yes, boss,' Tom responded, with not a little indifference. 'I must have lost it when I was rolling around the floor wrestling with that bloody gorilla.'

The Inspector was barely able to speak. 'You . . . you . . . can't just lose a bullet! These things have to be accounted for! Do you have any idea how important a single bullet is?'

Tom smiled. 'Well, *I* do, boss. But do *you*?'

Sadly, that was not an isolated incident. I once went with Mike at five in the morning to a briefing at a police station in the north end of the city. Apparently, a wages snatch had taken place at a local factory and the blaggers had used, and fired, a sawn-off shotgun. We had been called in because the local officers had been given two addresses at which it was expected we would find members of the gang.

Once the briefing was over, I went with Mike to

collect our weapons. Again, there were just the two of us. My own preference was for the snub-nosed, five-shot .38 Smith and Wesson Police Special, but instead the inspector in charge of arranging gun collections handed me the six-shot version.

'Where's the holster?' I asked him.

He looked up as if surprised I was still there. 'Haven't you got one?' he asked.

I shook my head.

'Well, use some string,' he added. To make matters worse, he had not arranged for Mike to be issued with a gun.

'What's going on?' I asked.

'The two addresses,' he answered in all seriousness, 'are close together in the same road. I don't see why you need two guns.'

There was nothing either Mike or myself could do about it, but before we left I turned back towards the inspector. 'Which address will you be at then, boss?' I asked.

'Neither,' he replied. 'I'll be here.'

'Wise move,' I said and walked out before he could collar me.

The two houses were about 200 yards apart and an anxious radio call caused me to sprint from one address to join Mike at the other. They had entered the house and found nobody, but the bedroom was locked. Our instructions to open up met with no response and so, having given fair warning that we were armed police officers, we forced the door.

Inside, we found a blagger hiding in the wardrobe with a large amount of cash and, lo and behold, a sawn-off shotgun. It was a good result but both Mike and myself were still furious over the allocation of firearms or, rather, the lack of it.

Chapter Three

At this time Mike and myself were seconded to a murder inquiry in Toxteth, following the brutal strangulation of a young prostitute. The Murder Control was set up at Lark Lane station, where I had been posted earlier in my service. Entering the general office, we were greeted by Superintendent Nat Sheron, who was running the show. He gave us an update on the current status of the investigation and related the most relevant details of the few statements already obtained.

I knew Nat well and he was a boss I had the highest regard for.

'You know this patch like the back of your hand, Mike,' he told me, 'so just hit the clubs and see what you can find out.'

We drove the short distance to Upper Parliament Street and, starting from the bottom, walked up the hill and entered each of the clubs in turn. Our first call was at the All Nations, followed by the El-Ah Ram, Dutch Eddie's, the Somali and the Federal. At each club we spoke to the owner and his staff, then mingled with the local prostitutes and punters whose faces were familiar to us.

Climbing the stairs of the Semi-Quaver club, we were

given a friendly greeting by the owner, Rudolph Gardener, known throughout the district as Bull. Quite a character, he was widely recognised as a respected community spokesman.

I was talking to him when Mike let out a low groan. 'Look what the wind's blown in.'

Following his gaze to the stairs, my heart sank.

Cathy was a local prostitute whose mood depended on the pills she had popped. She could be as meek as a pussycat or the most foul-mouthed, abusive, vicious of women. Fortunately, tonight was a good one. Particularly well dressed on this occasion, she was wearing a floppy straw sunhat with the most enormous brim.

We asked her about the murder and, though she knew nothing, she said she would contact us if she heard anything. With a quick 'Tarrah', she disappeared into the room that served as both the bar and disco.

It was nearly midnight when we were finished at the club, and, as we spoke to Bull by the front door, Cathy came weaving her way towards us, asking for a light. Mike obliged her and, as he raised his lighter to her cigarette, he was straining to listen to what Bull was trying to say above the racket of the disco.

Suddenly, there was a piercing scream followed by a torrent of foul language. Startled, I turned sharply and saw Cathy, incensed with fear and rage, desperately flapping at the flames leaping up above her head.

Mike, as he had given her a light, had accidentally set fire to her hat.

Once the flames were doused, she was none the worse for the experience, but she lunged at Mike and had to be manhandled out of the club by two of Bull's bouncers. She disappeared through the doorway, kicking her legs and screaming, a small trail of smoke still billowing over her head.

Once we were back in the car, it was a good twenty minutes before Mike or I could see through the tears of our hysterical laughter well enough to drive.

The murder was resolved within a day or so when the killer walked into Essex Street Police Station and confessed.

Cathy was always willing to help the police when she could, knowing how vulnerable were the women of her calling. They mixed with dangerous people and had the saddest and most weird of men among their customers. They also lived in a drug-infested world and many of the girls were addicts.

There was a strange relationship between us detectives and the girls. Both parties accepted the other as a necessary evil of life, rubbing shoulders as each in their own way worked the same streets. They knew we would never arrest them when we saw them soliciting, that was the responsibility of the Vice Squad. Because of this tacit understanding, when it suited both parties they could work together, primarily in such cases as the murder of one of their own. Personally, I never spoke down to any of these women; rather, I treated them with the respect that I would any other female. Who was I to sit in judgement over another human being's morals or life style? This attitude resulted in me getting a lot of valuable information from them.

A few weeks after the incident in the Semi-Quaver club we were called to Cathy's flat in Mulgrave Street, not far from Upper Parliament Street. Friends had reported that she had not been seen for a few days and there was no answer at her house. On arrival we managed to force entry through the back door. Mike found her sprawled on her bed. She had been dead for several days, but it was later revealed the cause of death was a combination of alcohol poisoning and a drug overdose. For all her faults, Cathy never did anyone any harm and I was saddened by the pathetic and lonely way she died.

Shortly afterwards, I was with Mike again when we drove onto the parking area alongside Speke Road Gardens in Garston, known locally (and sarcastically) as the Mansions. The 'gardens' were, in fact, another huge tenement block and we were regular visitors there.

On this occasion we were calling to speak to one of our regular informants who had telephoned earlier in the day asking us to visit. We were loath to leave the car unattended as we did not want to return and find the windows smashed and the tyres slashed. Mike stayed put and I made my way on my own to the man's top-floor flat.

His wife, Emma, answered my knock. She showed me into a small lounge, where her husband was eating fish, chips and peas from a plate balanced on his knee. He had obviously been drinking, but was keen to tell me about a man selling stolen car radios in the Mariners pub on St Mary's Road at the other end of Garston.

Emma entered the room and initially remained silent. Then she offered her opinion as to where the stolen radios may have come from. 'Well,' she said quietly, 'there's that place on the industrial estate by Evans Medical. That was broken into –'

'Shut yer mouth!' her husband bawled at her. He then crashed his plate of food over the woman's head.

Has Emma shown the slightest objection, I would have spoken up on her behalf. Instead, she sat in silence. I don't which of the two of us was the most embarrassed.

As she tried to maintain some degree of dignity, not easy with peas in your hair, her husband continued as if nothing had happened.

I was keen to remove myself and, after telling the man I would get back to him when I had checked out the information he had given me, I made my way to the door.

Emma showed me out and I could not help feeling sorry for her. 'I'm sorry about that,' I said, sympathetically. 'He was out of order. Would you like me to have a word with him?'

Opening the door, she shrugged. 'It's all right, Mr Mulloy,' she said with resignation. 'He'd only take it out on me later. But one day he'll go too far.'

A few weeks later, there was a vicious robbery at a warehouse in Speke. In the early hours of the morning, a security guard had disturbed three men loading up a van with stolen property. He was clubbed over the head with a baseball bat, kicked unconscious and left bleeding in a pool of his own blood.

Tom had been given the inquiry and Mike and I were on the case with him. After two days, we were getting nowhere.

On the third afternoon, Emma came into the station and asked to see me. She had a small suitcase with her and told me she was leaving her husband and taking the children to stay with her mother.

'There's one last thing I want to do before I go,' she said. She named her husband and two of his friends as being responsible for the warehouse robbery. Within a couple of hours, all three men were in police cells and were later given long prison sentences.

Emma had had her revenge.

Chapter Four

Just before six one Saturday morning, I met up with Mike at Lark Lane. For several weeks, we had been given the run-around by a prolific burglar who was wanted by a number of police forces around the country. Finally we had an address for him and, although it was supposed to be our rest day, we agreed to give him an early call.

Following a quick coffee, we were making our way out of the station when Eric McGonagle, the control room sergeant, called us back.

'Where are you off to, lads?' he asked.

'We're hitting a flat in Ullet Road,' Mike answered.

'Is it important? Allerton are going ape. They've got a suspected murder at the golf club and can't find any jacks. Can you help them out?' This was outside our division and normally we would not get involved in a case there.

Mike looked at me and we both shrugged. Our burglar would surface again before long.

'We're on our way,' I said.

A few minutes later we pulled into Allerton Golf Club, where several police panda cars were already in attendance. A local sergeant took us through to the murder scene not from far from the main gates.

Barbara was lying on her back with a scarf tightly fastened around her neck. Her skirt had been pulled up above her waist. I left Mike to make sure the course had been closed and the area was 'sterile'. This meant that no members of the public would be allowed access to the area and nobody, whoever they were, would be permitted to approach the body except by a predetermined path.

I went back to the car and, over the radio, called in those required to attend: a police surgeon, the CID chiefs, a coroner's officer and a Scene of Crime team to examine and photograph the area around the body.

The first to arrive was the divisional Detective Superintendent, Frank Jones, a man for whom I had the utmost respect. He listened intently to my briefing as I took him to look at the body.

Gordon McKenzie, deputy head of the CID, joined us a few moments later and put both Mike and myself on the case. And this was our rest day.

The Murder Control was set up at the nearby police training school on Mather Avenue and the first conference was held just before noon. Twenty detectives had been called in and, at his briefing, Gordon told us that over the weekend the inquiry was down to us. As this meant we would be working extended hours outside of our normal duties, headquarters had authorised it as a 'special occasion'. This meant we would be paid for each and every hour we worked.

We were given the task of talking to all known prostitutes in the area around Park Way, which ran between Parliament Street and Princes Road and was the heart of Toxteth's red-light district. Those girls worked unsociable hours and, subsequently, so did we. I had worked on a number of murders by now and knew that I could function without sleep for over forty-eight hours.

On the first night of the investigation we worked through to three in the morning and were back at Mather Avenue for the conference at nine. That night, we were out until three again and by the time we returned for Monday morning's conference more than sixty detectives had been drafted in to assist, but it was obvious from the partially shaved and bleary-eyed individuals who had worked the weekend. It was the same officers who groaned the loudest when the news was given that HQ had withdrawn the investigation's 'special occasion' status. We had been worked into the ground all weekend and then seen the carrot taken away. Nobody blamed Gordon. He had worked the same hours we had. It was another typical decision from the pen-pushers in Hope Street Headquarters.

The inquiry ran for some time and eventually a man was arrested. He was subsequently convicted and sentenced to life imprisonment.

A few months later I was roused from my bed in the early hours of a Sunday morning. Another woman had been murdered.

Just before midnight, Pauline, a 29-year-old mother of three, had staggered along Mulgrave Street. Falling into the gutter, she had bled to death from the stab wounds in her chest.

A massive manhunt for her killer began.

With Tom Hall, I spoke to a local girl named Jenny who was familiar with life on the streets and had called into the station in Lark Lane to tell of us an incident earlier in the week. She had picked up a client in the early hours of the morning and had gone with him down a back entry off Kingsley Road, a quarter of a mile from where Pauline had been murdered.

With her skirt hitched up around her waist, they had had sex standing up. When she'd thought they were finished, she had pulled down her skirt and prepared to leave (the street girls did not bother with knickers). Suddenly, the man had grabbed her and pulled a knife. For the next two hours he had sickeningly abused her and, when he was finally sated, he had taken back the money he had originally given her.

This was certainly someone we wanted to talk to and Jenny was sure she would recognise the man if ever she saw him again. Before Jenny left the station, we told her that if she spotted him, she should report it to one of the many officers patrolling the area and mention our names.

Incredibly, she was making her way home when she saw the man close to Sefton Park. Within minutes, the sorry individual was hauled into the station and was sitting before us. He immediately confessed to the assault on Jenny and broke down, full of remorse for his perverted actions. He was aged thirty and still lived with his parents in a respectable home in Aigburth. His encounter with Jenny was, he told us, his first sexual experience with a woman.

Some of my fellow officers had little or no sympathy when girls like Jenny were sexually assaulted. Both Tom and myself took a different view. The man was charged with indecent assault and theft and later pleaded guilty at the Crown Court.

Even Jenny was surprised when the man was

charged. She was only in her early thirties, but the life she led was reflected in every line on her face. As a single mother of three young children, she wasn't a full-time prostitute, neither was she afraid of hard work. But life was tough and she turned to the streets to supplement her income so that she could provide her kids with the things they needed.

Her regular job was as a barmaid in the Clock public house on Kingsley Road and, following this incident, Tom and I were always assured of a warm welcome when we dropped in. It was known as one of the toughest pubs in the city and I was amazed to discover when I first arrived at Lark Lane that it was a 'no go' area for police officers. I wasn't going to accept that and, after a few low-key visits, the regulars readily accepted me. Despite its reputation, the locals raised a lot of money for worthy causes and most were guilty of little more than bending a few rules to look after themselves and their own.

I even took Carol and Imelda there one night when I was invited to a charity event taking place in the pub. I introduced them to Jenny and noticed how pleased she seemed at the gesture. Despite the bravado she displayed to the outside world, deep down Jenny was ashamed and embarrassed by having to work the streets to survive. She was touched to be accepted as just an ordinary woman and an accepted member of our company.

Sadly, there was no happy ending for Jenny. Within a year she moved to another city, looking for a fresh start. Almost inevitably, she ended up back on the streets and was horrifically murdered. The subsequent trial and conviction of her killer was one of the longest in the history of British justice. She did not deserve to die that way, leaving behind the three young children who quite rightly adored her.

Some days into the inquiry on Pauline's murder, I was out driving along the streets with Mike, talking to anyone who might be able to help us. Close to Park Way, we saw a young woman standing in the shadows. Her face was familiar to us and I knew her to be an acquaintance of Barbara, the girl found on Allerton golf course.

We parked and got out of the car to talk to her, but she was immediately aggressive.

'You never caught the bastard who killed Barbara!' she screamed.

I glanced at Mike, a little puzzled, before answering, 'Yes, we did. He got life.'

'You bastard!' she screamed back at me. 'You're lying!' She then flung herself at me and raked at my face with her nails. I grabbed her by the arms but, even with Mike's help, had a hell of a job restraining her and getting her into the car. Even then, she promptly lashed out with her feet and kicked out the windscreen, which flew through the air in one piece before smashing on the ground.

We took her to the Main Bridewell in Cheapside, off Dale Street, in the city centre and told the duty inspector she had been arrested for assault.

'That's it?' he said, staring at me. 'Assault? Have you seen your face?' Checking in a mirror, I saw what he meant. Not only was the left side of my face badly lacerated, but my right cheek had also been torn open and the blood was gushing down my neck onto my shirt and jacket.

I looked at Mike, wondering why he had not said anything.

32

He shrugged. 'I didn't want to worry you.'

It transpired that it was not just the woman's nails that had raked my face. In her left hand she had been clutching a bunch of keys.

The woman was charged with wounding and I eventually got to bed after dawn with several sutures for company. Shortly after nine, Carol woke me to say my dad was on the phone and needed to speak to me urgently. Still half asleep, I was a little puzzled when he asked me if I was all right.

'Yes,' I answered, 'why wouldn't I be?'

'It was on the local news you'd been stabbed,' he said.

A local radio station had reported on its hourly news bulletin that Detective Sergeant Mike Mulloy had been stabbed in the face in Toxteth and that a young woman had been arrested and was helping police with their inquiries. I had told him the news item had been exaggerated but he would not rest until he had spoken to me personally. My mother had died of a stroke in 1967 when she was just fifty-five. Our grief had brought us all closer together and Dad was understandably protective towards Imelda and myself.

The Pauline inquiry lasted several seeks but, despite the hard work, it was eventually closed down. It was the first murder inquiry I had worked on not to come to a successful conclusion. I felt deflated and depressed. Pauline's murderer was still walking the streets – Pauline had not been avenged.

Chapter Five

Driving out of the city centre in the early hours of the morning, a message came over the radio that burglars had been disturbed at a factory off Mill Street in the Dingle, a small working-class area sandwiched between Toxteth, Aigburth and the river.

We pulled up outside the main entrance of the factory and ran to the rear as uniformed officers gathered at the front. Almost immediately, Tom spotted two men on the roof.

'Let's get up there,' Tom said.

This was easier said than done. The roof was some sixty feet up with no obvious means of access. When Tom called up to the two men, they showed no inclination to come down, so he sent for the fire brigade.

Within a few minutes, two fire engines arrived, one of which was hydraulic platform as requested.

The sub-officer in charge, with two silver bars across his shoulders, approached us. 'What can we do for you?' he said to Tom. Although we were all in plain clothes, Tom was clearly the senior officer of the three of us. He pointed to the roof.

'Can you put me and my lads up there?' he asked,

pointing to the section of the roof where the two men had last been seen.

'In the blink of an eye,' the sub-officer answered confidently.

Once the fire engine's stabilisers were in place, the fireman operating the ladder electronically told us to climb up to the top of the first section. 'Hold on tight,' he suggested with a smile, 'and I'll give you a lift the rest of the way.'

Standing immediately below Tom, I held on for dear life as the ladder was slowly raised towards the roof. This was obviously entertaining for the two firemen watching below. Spending half their lives running up and down ladders, they must have found our anxiety amusing.

When the ladder came to a halt, we were a few feet above the level of what was, thankfully, a flat roof, but a yard or two away from it.

'Can you jump from there?' one of the firemen shouted up.

'Very blood funny!' I shouted back.

There was a chorus of chuckles from below but, a few seconds later, the ladder was moved in towards the edge of the roof and came to a stop a few inches short of it. We immediately stepped off and found the two men within a minute, hiding in the darkness.

'What's happening, lads?' I asked them.

'Came up here for a piss, didn't we?' one answered, with resignation.

Shortly, the uniformed lads were flashing their torches around the darker recesses and quickly found a jemmy and a door that had been forced open. The men were nicked.

A few months later, the pair who had opted to be tried by 'a jury of their peers', pleaded not guilty at the Crown Court, which in those days was in the St George's Hall on Lime Street. I had to attend the trial and was the first prosecution witness to be called. As I was cross-examined, all was going well until I was asked to describe the lay-out of the roof. I couldn't. I explained to the judge that it was dark and I had not been carrying a torch. I did not add that my lack of enthusiasm for heights might have added to my confusion.

This was a detail that was apparently important to the case for the defence and the counsel for the accused insisted it was imperative the site be viewed if he were to demonstrate his clients' innocence. The judge accepted his petition and ordered that a visit be made to the scene. That afternoon a single-decker bus, hired for the purpose, pulled up outside the court and judge, jury, barristers, accused, police witnesses and ushers climbed on board to make the short journey to Mill Street.

When the bus arrived at our destination, there was a car park where the factory should have been. In the months since the arrests had been made, the building had been demolished. I looked across at the two accused men as they openly smirked. Being local lads, they knew well enough the factory had been bulldozed and saw an opportunity for the case to be dismissed on a technicality.

They nearly succeeded. The defence argued that a vital part of their case related to the lay-out of the roof, and both Tom and Mike had a hard time when they followed me into the witness box. The case was proved but our two likely lads walked free on probation, making their way straight to the Legs of Man public house at the bottom of London Road for a celebratory drink.

I was not the most popular figure as we trundled back to the station in silence.

'OK,' I said, wounded by this silent rebuke. 'In future, I'll drive around the city and make a note of all the buildings being knocked down.' In the early sixties, great parts of the city were being cleared and my suggestion was obviously sarcastic. But I made my point.

In the early hours of one morning, I was called to the casualty department of Sefton General Hospital on Smithdown Road. I knew Sister Lorna Hughes in charge of the unit and we got on well. She explained that, a short while earlier, a young woman had been brought into the hospital in a private vehicle but was found to be 'dead on arrival'.

The Sister told me that she had been brought in by a young man who had apparently found her unconscious on Queens Drive, near Menlove Avenue, a short drive from the hospital. Her death was not obviously suspicious but, as I peered through the venetian blinds of the Sister's office, I saw the man pacing anxiously backwards and forwards.

'Why did you call me in?' I asked, turning back towards Lorna.

'I wasn't going to at first,' she said. 'There are no signs of wounds and the man's account seemed plausible. He was a little agitated, but then he had just found a dead body. I suppose he's entitled to be upset.'

'So what changed your mind?'

'One of the nurses undressing the body called me in.

The woman's brassiere was only partially fastened and her skirt wasn't buttoned properly.'

'Maybe she was in a hurry when she dressed,' I suggested.

'Perhaps,' the Sister answered. 'But that's not all. Her knickers were inside out. She's been dressed by someone else.'

I went with her to have a look at the body of what had been a very attractive woman and found that there was no indication of assault or injury. But something was not right. 'I'm not happy with the state of her clothing, especially the underwear.'

The Sister nodded. 'That's what I thought.'

Next, I talked to the man in the Sister's office and, almost immediately, his account was riddled with inconsistencies.

I leaned back in my seat and looked hard at him. 'You're a liar,' I said firmly. 'I am concerned that you may well have played a part in the death of this young woman. I want the truth and I want it now.'

'Oh, Jesus!' he suddenly blurted. 'Oh, sweet Jesus, I never killed no one!' He broke down in tears and the sorry tale came spilling out. 'I'm a married man but I've been asking that girl to go out with me for weeks. In the end she said she would. I took her to a pub where no one would know me.'

'Where?'

'God, I don't even know. I just drove out into the country until we came to a pub. Somewhere out near Frodsham, I guess.'

'Go on.'

'We had a few drinks and left. On the way home, I

parked up in a secluded little lane and we started neckin'
and that. You know how it is. Anyway, she was up for it,
so we climbed into the back of the car and got
undressed.' He hesitated and looked up at me, but I
nodded for him to continue.

'Well, we were doin' it, you know, having sex, and
she's making a lot of noise, like, well, you know, when
suddenly . . . oh, sweet Jesus!' He raised his hands to his
face and sobbed. 'Suddenly, she makes this scary,
gargling noise and collapses. For a second, I thought she
was messing about, but then I knew she wasn't. I knew
she was dead. I didn't know what to do. I didn't even
know where I was. I just dressed her and drove back to
Liverpool. Once I got me bearings, I drove her here.'

Shortly afterwards I attended the post-mortem which
confirmed that she had died from a massive brain
haemorrhage and the man was in the clear. But, though
I was now convinced his account was more or less true,
I was not impressed by his reaction to the news.

'Does that mean I can go? You don't have to tell me
wife?'

'As she died of natural causes, there probably won't
be an inquest.'

'Oh, thank God,' he said.

'I'm not sure what God would make of it,' I told him,
'but you could spare a thought for the dead girl.'

Nodding frantically, he turned and walked into the
night. I wondered what his wife would make of his mood
when he got home.

A few weeks later, just after midnight, I was at the
same casualty unit. The uniform duty inspector had

telephoned and asked me to look into a report of a shooting incident. A young man had been brought in to the hospital by ambulance, suffering from a serious shotgun wound to his thigh. He told me that he would meet up with me there.

When I spoke to the young man, his version of events was obviously far divorced from the truth. He had, he said, been walking along the road when two men had approached him. Without motive or warning, one of the men had pulled out a shotgun and blasted him in the leg. He said they then ran off and he had crawled to the local police station, the best part of half a mile away.

I doubted he could have crawled so far without collapsing with pain or loss of blood. I also thought it unlikely he could cover such a distance so slowly through a well-populated area without coming across someone who would have helped him.

'Listen, pal,' I said, with serious scepticism, 'I may have been born at night, but not last night. The fairy tale was very good. Now tell me what really happened.'

He quickly acknowledged the futility of lying and a more plausible account of the evening's events followed. With two friends, he had been out poaching on the farms dotted around Speke. They were each carrying a loaded shotgun. One of his friends had tripped and accidentally discharged his gun, hitting the man lying before me in the leg. As they did not want to be prosecuted, they had concocted their fantastic story, driven him nearly all the way to the local police station and left him to stagger the last few yards.

Within an hour, the other two men had been traced and the three shotguns had been seized. Inevitably, the men did not have a licence for them. With that, as far as I was concerned, the matter was closed. The Firearms Department would make any decisions regarding the guns.

I was booking the guns into the property system at the police station when the duty inspector entered. He made some blustering excuse for not attending the hospital but, knowing him as I did, it had never once occurred to me that he would show up. He was one of those officers who liked to present an air of efficiency and authority but who, in reality, walked in the opposite direction when anything serious turned up.

In answer to his query, I briefly related what had actually occurred.

'I hope you booked them for poaching,' he said, haughtily.

I shook my head and walked away without answering.

Chapter Six

One late November afternoon, Mike and I were prowling about the city in an unmarked car with no particular purpose in mind other than to uncover mischief. We responded to a call from a jeweller's shop in London Road in the city centre, where a man had tendered an Access credit card that the manager suspected was stolen. The man carrying the card was still on the premises.

We arrived at the shop a couple of minutes later and Mike stayed by the door as I spoke briefly to members of the staff and took the card. The man they pointed out was nonchalantly looking at some display cases, apparently oblivious to my presence.

'CID, pal,' I said, approaching him. 'Is this your card?'

'Yeah, that's right,' he answered, confidently.

'What name is it?'

'Paul McCarron.'

'Can you spell that for me?' I smiled as he gave McCarron a double n instead of a double r. 'Nice try, pal, but you're nicked.'

He shrugged and made no protest as I led him from the shop and put him into the back seat of the car.

He gave us his real name and, as Mike turned into the traffic, he spoke again. 'I know two fellas with a sawn-off shotgun who are going to do a job.'

'Sounds interesting,' I said, 'but you can tell us all about that later. First, we're going to our office.'

On arrival at the Crime Squad office he was again cautioned and asked if he was responsible for any other offences using this card.

'No, but let me tell you about the shooters.'

I told him that we intended to take him to his flat to search it, and after that we would talk about the guns.

'I'd better tell you. I've got the gun but it might not be in the flat.'

This put a new complexion on things.

'Why not?'

'I've got an arrangement with my flatmate that if I don't make regular meets with him during the day he's to unload it. I was supposed to see him in town at two o'clock this afternoon.'

We travelled to his flat and, on arrival, we parked up outside and tried to decide whether or not to apply for assistance before we entered.

'Where's the shotgun?'

'In a bag. I'll show you.'

'Can anyone get to it when we go in? Is your mate likely to give us trouble?'

'The gun may be out, there's ammunition for it. You can never tell.'

It was hardly the kind of reassurance we were looking for. If his mate was watching from the window, he could be waiting for us when we went in.

'What do you reckon?' Mike asked me.

'It's too late to bring in armed back-up,' I replied. 'Shall we go for it?'

'We've got no choice,' Mike said. 'But let's hit it fast before I change my mind.'

Within a minute, we were outside the front door of the flat.

Mike gave me a nod, turned the key and we both burst into the flat, shouting 'Police!' as if our lives depended on it. For all we knew, they did.

We saw the flatmate immediately and, much to our relief, he froze. A quick search of the premises resulted in us finding not only the sawn-off shotgun and five rounds of live ammunition, but also a replica handgun in a holster.

We spent the rest of the evening interviewing Jennings. Initially he confessed to buying the shotgun a week earlier and to hiring it out to an unknown villain he had met in a pub. Both Mike and I knew that such a weapon would only be hired for one purpose: an armed blag.

He continued to trip himself up in the same vein and, eventually, he admitted using the handgun himself with another man when attempting to rob a butcher's shop of its takings a few days earlier. His accomplice had attacked the shopkeeper with a hammer, but the man had fought back bravely with a cleaver and the two had fled empty-handed. By now we also had an associate of his in custody. This man confessed that they were conspiring to carry out a string of armed robberies over the next few days. The next job would have been on business premises the following week, when they intended tying up the staff and taking the money he knew would be there. They'd also been watching shopkeepers drop their takings at a number of cash points and had calculated the best time to make an attack.

Early in the evening, as Mike progressed the inquiry, I slipped back over the water to St Catherine's Hospital. Carol had been admitted to the maternity unit a day or so earlier as she was having problems with her first pregnancy. Some days later she lost the baby we were both so desperate for. It was a crushing blow for us, made worse by the fact that it was only three days before her birthday and three weeks before Christmas.

By the end of the day, Jennings was charged with illegal possession of a firearm, attempted robbery and several counts of conspiracy to rob. Two of his accomplices were also in custody and facing similar charges. Given his confession, the case against him seemed cut and dried, but I knew from bitter experience that the more straightforward a case appeared to be, the more likely it was that there would be problems in court.

Jennings appeared before the Recorder of Liverpool, Judge Rudolph Lyons, and pleaded not guilty to all the counts against him. At the trial, John Briggs appeared for the Crown and Jack Cowan defended Jennings.

The trial lasted eight days and a collection of serious allegations flew around the court, including the accusation that Mike and I had beaten the confession out of Jennings. It was a question of who the jury would believe, but the case ended in a way I have never seen before or since.

Part of Jennings's defence was that he had found the sawn-off shotgun when he first moved into the flat. He said he knew nothing about guns and had kept it

45

because he thought it was an antique. I had to admit he was impressive in the witness box and could not be shaken. He had finished giving his evidence when Judge Lyons asked him a question.

'Can you enlighten me? I see that a hole has been drilled through the stock of the weapon. What's that for?'

'When you shorten a shotgun it makes the recoil much greater. So you drill the hole and put a strap through so that when you fire it you can . . .'

His voice suddenly trailed off as the horror of what he had said struck him. From the collective gasp that went up from the jury box, they had certainly not missed the relevance of what he had said. If he was an innocent with firearms how could he possibly have known that?

Judge Lyons allowed a defence request for a further consultation with Jennings at this point. He then changed his plea to guilty and received five and a half years imprisonment. In the countless trials that I have been involved with none has ever ended in such a dramatic fashion.

Nat Sheron was a boss who liked getting out from behind his desk and on to the streets as often as possible. Late one evening he parked in Upper Parliament Street, intending to have a wander around the area. As he was locking his car he noticed a group of young men standing nearby. Suddenly one approached him, pulled out a knife and demanded his wallet. He had made one hell of a mistake with Nat who immediately grappled with him. He managed to squirm out of Nat's grasp and ran off while the other youths scattered in all directions.

I was on night duty and, having heard about the

incident when I came on duty, I immediately visited the clubs in the area. I spoke to all the owners and expressed my extreme displeasure over the affair. It was an unusual occurrence. Detectives were all well known in the district and it was inconceivable that an attempt would be made to rob one, more so the most senior CID officer in the division. I left the definite impression that this was one job that would be detected, come what may.

I obviously got the message across that I meant business. A couple of hours later an anonymous telephone call was received and I was directed to go to a telephone kiosk in Kingsley Road as soon as possible. As I drove up I saw about half a dozen men standing outside the kiosk. I was a little apprehensive but the men melted into the shadows as I got out of the car. Inside the box was a solitary figure. I opened the door and the young man surrendered himself to me as being the person responsible for the attempted robbery.

I arrested him and discovered that he was from Manchester, which explained why he had not recognised Nat. He was already circulated as wanted for a similar offence in the Salford area of that city and he had come to Liverpool to avoid arrest. Obviously the locals had decided that the trouble that may come their way could be avoided and had taken the matter into their own hands.

As a result of dealing with this arrest, it was far later than usual when I walked into the canteen at a station in the city centre. I apologised to the young women waiting to serve me and asked if there were any meals left.

'Certainly, Mr Mulloy – fish, steak, whatever you like.'
'I'm sorry, have I met you before?'

'Not really. You dealt with me brother. He got six years for robbery.'

My appetite vanished and I settled for a cup of coffee and a packet of biscuits. In my imagination I could see all manner of unspeakable things happening to my dinner out of my sight!

Had I chosen a meal I would not have had time to enjoy it. Minutes later I was on my way to meet Detective Inspector Ken Anderson at a flat a short distance from Lark Lane station. Ken was a good boss who I always enjoyed working with. On arrival, the uniformed officer guarding the door directed me to a bedroom where I found Ken. A 52-year-old woman was lying on her back on the bed, which was heavily soaked in blood. What fascinated me was the handle of a large kitchen knife protruding from the woman's chest.

Our examination revealed that the knife had been thrust right through her body and into the mattress. Considerable force must have been used to cause such a dreadful wound.

The murder was not hard to detect as it was a domestic killing. Her husband, a mild-mannered clerk, had already walked into Lark Lane and told the desk officer what he had done. When he was interviewed I found it incredible that this harmless-looking fellow was capable of such ferocity. What's more, the slaughter which had led to an early grave was the result of a mundane row.

Chapter Seven

On a summer's afternoon a shopkeeper left his grocery premises in Toxteth to collect money from the bank. As he drove off, he noticed three men sitting in a dark blue Cortina almost opposite his shop but thought little of it. Having collected his cash, he was turning into Upper Parliament Street when his vehicle was rammed head-on by the Cortina. The three men jumped out and tried to drag him from his car, screaming for him to give them his money. By chance, a patrolling police car came across the scene. The three would-be robbers fled, pursued by two constables, who managed to catch one of them. A large crowd had gathered and they, in turn, attacked the officers and released their prisoner. Both constables were beaten and kicked as they lay on the pavement, but fortunately escaped any serious injury.

Mike and I took charge of the investigation but all we had to go on were the descriptions of the attackers. None of them were known, even by sight, by the officers or the victim of this terrifying incident. The car used in the raid had been stolen earlier that day from Princes Avenue. We hit the streets and began to ask questions. Later that night we were in George's club in Upper

Parliament Street making our presence known, but nobody was saying anything. Sarah, a nineteen-year-old prostitute was drinking in the club. As she got up to leave she caught my eye and indicated with her head that we should follow her. A few moments later we did so and she led us into a dark side alley.

'It's David Swailes you want for that job, Mr Mulloy. I saw him driving the Cortina just before the job came down.'

'OK, Sarah, that's good. There should be some cash in this for you.'

'No, I don't want nothin'. He's a bastard and, anyway, I already owe you one.' Sarah was out on the game every night without fail. She had a small son and this was her way of supplementing her income to give him the best life that she could. Some weeks earlier, a uniformed constable had found her engaged in a furious row with a client in his car on some wasteland. He alleged to the constable that Sarah had stolen money from his pocket while they were having sex. They had both been brought to Lark Lane and Tom and I were called to deal with the matter. Though I may have doubted Sarah's morals, I was convinced that she was no thief.

The client was a man in his forties whom I took an instant dislike to. His attitude was patronising and at first he attempted to talk down to us. He got little sympathy. The vehicle had been searched and no money had been found. The only cash in Sara's possession was that which even the client agreed he had paid her. We strongly suspected that this was a ruse by the client, either to get his money back or divert attention from him being found in the company of a prostitute. We took him into a side office where he was insistent that the theft be prosecuted.

'OK, but we'll have to take a witness statement from you.'

'I've just told you what happened.'

'We will need it for the court case.'

'Will I have to go to court?'

'Of course. The girl is denying the theft, so you will have to give evidence.'

'Will it be in the papers?'

'Who can say? We have no control over such things.'

Suddenly his whole manner changed.

'I've been thinking – I may be mistaken about this after all.'

'Really. Are you married?'

'Yes, I am.'

'Take some explaining to your wife, I suppose, getting caught screwing a teenager.'

Within minutes he had changed his mind completely about the situation and was on his way out of the nick having dropped his allegation. We went through to the interview room to see Sarah.

'Come on, love, let's get you home to see your baby.'

'D'you really believe me? Can I go?'

'Yes, Sarah, right now. Come on, we'll give you a lift.'

'Thanks, gents, I'm really grateful.'

Now we had received the benefit of that gratitude. In the early hours of the morning we hit Swailes's flat in Kingsley Road. We took no chances and simply kicked his door in. A big muscular man, he went absolutely berserk in his efforts to escape. He was a real handful. After a violent battle we eventually got him on the floor and restrained him. Once he realised there was nowhere to go, he gave it up. On interview he at first tried to deny everything. However, he was not stupid. Faced with the prospect of being identified by the constables who had caught him, and his victim, he eventually admitted his part in the attack. Later that morning he was charged and kept in custody. He already had a record and we objected to him being granted bail but he was released on a subsequent appearance before the magistrates.

Other events soon brought him back to mind. Upper Parliament Street is the main arterial road that divides Toxteth and runs through to the city centre. The lower part by Parkway was the red-light district of Liverpool and contained many clubs. People came to the area from all over the city and from far afield, many for the purpose of illicit sex. Obviously, this meant that many were carrying substantial amounts of money. Because of this, the area was notorious for street robberies. These were cowardly, vicious and difficult to detect. Detectives working the ground accepted this as a fact of life.

Over some months, a disturbing pattern began to emerge that these robberies were escalating, both in number and in the degree of gratuitous violence being used. Invariably there would be three attackers, often carrying knives, and we had to assume that many robberies were not being reported, for obvious reasons. We knew we had a serious problem on our hands. Nat Sheron took Mike and me off normal inquiries and instructed us to concentrate solely on these crimes. We took overall responsibility for the investigation.

We made several arrests for some of the robberies but still they continued.

Several times Swailes was mentioned as being involved but, despite all our endeavours, we had no evidence to connect him. His previous conviction was similar to the pattern we were investigating but that was not unusual. The breakthrough came from an unexpected source.

In the early hours of the morning a 37-year-old man engaged the services of a young prostitute who took him to her home nearby. Afterwards, as he returned to his car, he was attacked by three men and punched and kicked to the ground. He was then dragged into an entry and stripped of his cash and valuables. He managed to stagger back to his car and report the incident at Lark Lane. It was the lead that we had been looking for. The man had so enjoyed his encounter with the girl that he had made a note of her flat number in case he wished to use her services again. Within minutes, Mike and I were banging on her door.

She was unknown to us and, initially, was most uncooperative. We suspected that she might have been used as bait to lure the victim to the scene. Eventually she admitted that she had been with the client and, as there was nothing else forthcoming, we prepared to leave. I gave her my name and asked that if she heard anything to let me know.

'Are you Mr Mulloy?'

'That's right.'

'Did you deal with Sarah when that client tried to set her up?'

'Yes, why?'

'She's me mate. She told me what you did for her and that you can be trusted.'

'That's nice of her. Give her my regards.'

'I haven't told you everything. It's Swailes that you want for this job.'

She gave us the lot then. After her client had left, she had heard a disturbance. She was afraid to go outside but had looked through the window. She had witnessed the attack and positively identified Swailes as the main aggressor. Obviously she was not prepared to make a statement as she had to live around there, but this was as good as it got.

Once again, we were dragging Swailes from his bed before dawn. He must have recalled our first encounter and this time there was no fighting. For a shrewd robber he had made a great mistake. He was wearing the client's inscribed watch on his wrist. During several lengthy interviews he admitted well over a hundred street robberies in less than a year. He marked on a map of the area where the attacks had taken place and was able to give us surprisingly accurate details of the offences.

Even though these were serious crimes, we had to smile over three files we pulled from the records, all concerning the same victim. On three consecutive Fridays this man had attended the same club only to be robbed each time at knifepoint in the toilet! I sympathised with the views of the detective who had dealt with the incidents. He could not believe that anyone could be so stupid and had suggested that the attacks were pure fiction.

Eventually we were ready to charge Swailes with a number of offences.

'Am I getting bail?'

'Do me a favour – no way.'

'It's better that I stay in, I just can't stop.'

'You popping pills or what?'

'It's just me way of life now. I've got to stop before someone gets hurt.'

Having seen some of his terrified and battered victims, what could he have meant by 'getting hurt'? The inquiries continued and two other men were arrested in connection with the series of robberies. On their appearance at the Crown Court all went down for several years. Swailes accepted his fate but his companions did not. They showed their true nature when a violent fight broke out in the dock and they had to be removed, struggling and swearing, to begin their sentences.

Unbeknown to me, Nat had written me up for this series of arrests and other investigations that I had been involved in. Some weeks later I was informed that I was to receive the coveted Award of Merit. This was a unique honour bestowed by the Police Watch Committee. They were a body consisting of magistrates and councillors with the responsibility for overseeing the policing of the city. It was a citation that was rarely awarded and the recipient has the privilege of wearing the insignia on their uniform. I was proud to join the ranks of the select few who had received it.

By a lovely coincidence I was to receive the award on Carol's birthday. At this stage I was attending a residential course at the training school. I had hardly attended any of the classes, due to being engaged in a number of trials at the Crown Court. I was halfway through one such case, a robbery, and the defence agreed that I could be released to collect my commendation.

I made my way to the municipal offices and found a sergeant from the personnel department awaiting me. He explained that, when my name was called, I was to enter the chamber where I would find Deputy Chief Constable Dalzell. A few minutes later I was ushered in. The DCC read out the citation and I was embarrassed as it was so flattering. He informed the assembly that my enthusiasm, ability and devotion to duty were an inspiration to my colleagues. He highlighted three inquiries, which had resulted in a number of arrests, and concluded that these cases were only a sample of my work. He also cited the many letters of appreciation that had been received from members of the public.

The Chairman of the Authority congratulated me and handed over my award. The emblem consisted of an embroidered Liver bird encircled with silver thread. I left the room and was still examining my trophy when the sergeant approached me again.

'Can I have it back, Mike?'

'What do you want it for?'

'We've only got the one, so I was told to get it back!'

'Wrong – you've got none now.'

Later that night, Carol and I had to attend the offices of the *Liverpool Post* and *Echo* to be photographed and interviewed. This was a nuisance as it delayed us for the restaurant I had booked to celebrate her birthday. By the time that I had enjoyed my meal I had put the ceremony out of my mind.

The following day I made my way from home to attend the Crown Court. I went to pay my parking fee but the attendant refused to take my money. I asked him why not.

'Least I can do. I'll make sure your car is OK.'

Somewhat puzzled, I made my way to St George's Hall. As I climbed the steps, a court usher who knew my father greeted me. My father had now retired as a decorator and had become an usher at the complex.

'Morning, Mike, I'll bet your dad's so proud he can't get his head through the door here today.'

'Proud of what?'

'Haven't you seen the morning papers?' he asked, handing me a copy.

The story and picture of Carol and me was plastered across the front of the morning issue, as it was to be in the evening edition. At least I now knew why the attendant had acted as he had.

The barrister for the defence in the case I was embroiled in must have thought things were going badly for his client. He cheekily asked for the case to be retried as the publicity might have had an adverse effect on the jury! The judge was not impressed.

Chapter Eight

One night I met up with an informant in the Greenhills pub in Allerton. He was waiting at the bar for me and, as I was getting in the drinks, he asked if I knew Tony Craven. Taking my change from the barman, I told him that I had dealt with him before.

'You know he's on the run from prison then?'

'Didn't even know he was inside.'

'You won't believe this. About three months ago he did a runner from an open prison.'

'Know where's he's staying?'

'Better than that. He's working as a coach driver. He only drives the bloody coach that picks up prisoners from the remand centre every day and takes them to court!'

'You're joking!'

I thought that I had heard most things but this was a new one on me. The next morning Mike and I were waiting as a coach entered the remand centre. The heavy doors closed behind it and there was the escaped prisoner, bright as a button, behind the wheel. His smile waned when he glanced over and saw us in the security office. The coach would be late for court that day.

The next information from this contact was far more

valuable. We met him in the same pub and what he had to tell us gripped our attention immediately. He mentioned the names of a gang of burglars whom he said were very active. Three of those names were only too well known to us. They had been the leaders of a team of housebreakers who were among the most prolific that I had ever encountered. We had arrested them three years before but only after they had gone on a rampage of crime in south Liverpool. When they had eventually appeared before the courts they had admitted responsibility for well in excess of a hundred burglaries. Now, it seemed, they were out and had gone straight back to crime.

Our source revealed that the gang were breaking into several houses of a night. According to him, they were operating in the Grassendale, Allerton, Childwall and Mossley Hill areas of the city. We were eventually to find that they had also travelled to Cheshire and Lancashire to commit crime. They always operated in a team of at least three and used stolen cars on their travels. Our informant was unable to tell us where they were living as they were keeping a low profile, having learnt lessons from the time we had arrested them. Having dealt with them before, we were aware that these were men who placed great importance on meticulous planning and were capable of extreme violence should the need arise.

Personally, I despised housebreakers. On many occasions I had dealt with people who could not bear to live in their homes after a burglary. The sense of violation in many cases cannot be adequately measured for the victims. Women in particular are affected; they feel that their privacy has been violated and can never feel the same about their beloved homes again. Old people can be especially vulnerable and often feel unable to leave their homes or sleep properly after an attack.

I have often been sorely tempted to punch the face of a burglar who, on being arrested, has sneered 'They're insured, aren't they?' This from the mouth of someone with no conscience and no conception of the harm he has done to a vulnerable person. What insurance money can replace the loss of a late mother's engagement ring, or of other treasured family possessions? How much money would it take to return someone's peace of mind after that home has been ransacked, a woman's underwear rifled through and, often, excreta left on the carpets and beds? House burglars are, in my opinion, among the lowest forms of criminal life.

Our inquiries at the divisions concerned backed up my informant's information. Someone had been cutting a swathe of crime through the night, and the patterns of the jobs were just right for these guys. The crimes had started about three months ago, and despite being disturbed on several occasions, the burglars had escaped. One householder had been assaulted in the early hours of the morning when he tried to detain one of them.

Armed with this information, we held a conference with Nat Sheron who commanded the division most affected by the crime wave. Our main problem was that we could not 'house' the burglars, as our informant did not know where they were living. However, we knew who they were and if they were on the streets at night it was just possible our paths would cross. We decided to start night-time patrols. It was not the most brilliant of plans but it was all that we could come up with. The only question was when to start. I looked at my watch and saw that by now it was mid-afternoon. We decided to call it a day and start that night, striking while the iron was hot.

Just after ten, we met at the office and drove to the target area in an unmarked police car. For several hours we criss-crossed the division but it was one of those nights when the radio was practically silent. Just before dawn, a wave of tiredness began to affect us and we were about to give it up and get some sleep. I suggested one last sweep and, as we approached Speke Road Gardens, through the night binoculars I saw a young man about to walk into the complex. Mike swung the car about and we gave him a pull just as he was about to vanish into the gloom of the block. As we neared him he put his right arm behind his back. I jumped out of the car and grabbed hold of him.

'CID officers – what's that in your hand?'

'Nothing.'

Mike pulled his hand out and discovered he was holding a bunch of Ford car keys.

'What's this, pal?'

'Just found them, didn't I?'

'Just found you, didn't we? Get in the car!'

At first the reason he gave for being out so late was that he was having an affair with a married woman. According to him, her husband worked nights at the Ford car factory. There was something about him that was not quite right. This man had not been mentioned by our contact, but our suspicions reached a high level when he admitted that he was an associate of several of those we were seeking. We decided to chance our hand. Our interest in them could get back to our targets; equally, we could have stumbled on to a gold mine. We arrested him for being in possession of the car keys with intent to commit a crime and drove to Speke Police Station to conduct a thorough interview.

Sometimes your luck is in, as in this case. During questioning it became apparent that our suspect was heavily involved with the men we were looking for. It became a battle of wits and we could not be certain exactly what he had done. We raised the subject of the householder who had been attacked. Suddenly we got the breakthrough we were seeking.

'I wasn't involved in that job.'

'Nobody said you were. But you know about it – you're at it with the same team.'

'I haven't done any at night.'

'OK, what have you been doing with them?'

'I screwed some houses in the daytime.'

'How many?'

'About ten, I think.'

'Where are the houses you broke into?'

'We done them mostly in the roads off Aigburth Road.'

'What was the last one?'

'A big house in the Serpentine two days ago.'

'How did you get in?'

'We used a spade that was in the garden and forced the back window with it.'

'What time was that?'

'Early afternoon. We had a drink in the Kingsman at lunch, then did the house.'

'What did you rob from the house?'

'We got about fifty quid, two tellies, a stereo and some jewellery.'

Mike went to check the records and, when he returned, he confirmed that such a break-in had indeed taken place.

'The only difference is that over a thousand pounds went, not fifty.'

'The thievin' bastards,' he exclaimed indignantly, 'they must have pocketed that themselves!'

There was no holding him back then; it all came tumbling out. He was so incensed at being cheated out of what he considered his rightful share, he was now only too glad to help. Part of his role in the crimes had been to steal the cars the gang would use. He was having the affair as he had told us, which was why he did not take part in the nocturnal burglaries. He admitted that when we had picked him up he was wandering around ready to steal a car. He was also able to give us the addresses of the main men that we wanted.

It was just before dawn when Mike and I left the station to obtain search warrants for the houses we were going to hit. We had called Tom out and he remained at the station trying to scrape up some manpower to assist us. As active detectives we knew where we could obtain warrants, even at this unearthly hour. We drove through the deserted streets to the fringes of the city centre. We knew that a newsagent, who was a local magistrate, would be at his shop marking his early morning papers. On entering the shop we spoke to his wife behind the counter and told her the purpose of our visit. Asking us to wait, she vanished into the rear of the shop and, within a minute or so, came back and invited us to go through. We did so but at first the office seemed deserted. Then a voice came from behind a closed door in the corner.

'All rights, lads, who is it?'

'DS Mulloy and DC Johnson. Sorry to bother you but we need some search warrants signing.' I then briefly outlined our investigation.

'That's fine lads, just shove them under the door!'

Somewhat incredulously I did so and they were signed and returned to us in the same manner. Mike picked them up and, thanking the disembodied voice, we left the shop. Sitting in our car, I waited while Mike checked that all the warrants were in order.

'D'you want to have a double-check, Mike?'

'No thanks,' I replied, 'you picked them up. The guy was sitting on the bog and hadn't washed his hands!'

Mike's response was quite colourful, but he did take pleasure in having Tom examine them on our return to Speke!

The first address we hit was in Central Way, a short drive from the station. This was the ringleader, the man we most wanted. In his mid-twenties and steeped in crime since his early teens, Jimmy Bell could best be described as a professional burglar. We had dealt with him before – he was probably one of the most prolific thieves I ever encountered.

We gained access to the house and Bell attempted to escape. A running battle took place throughout the house but eventually he was overpowered and arrested. A search of the house resulted in the recovery of a large quantity of stolen property from burgled homes, and by the time Nat Sheron came on duty, we already had four men in custody. He was also in time to save us from the unwelcome attention of a particular inspector from the station. We had used his office to do the initial interview and I must confess we did it leave it in a mess, with coffee mugs, ashtrays and files strewn about. He was not amused at what he found when he entered the CID office later that morning.

Tom had been rushing about and had brought one detained man to the station. As he was anxious to join us for the next raid, he left his prisoner under the watchful eye of a detective who was doing some paperwork and, before leaving, he handcuffed him to a radiator. It was some hours before we returned with more prisoners and stolen goods to find awaiting us the very irate inspector. Tom had forgotten that the central heating system was due to come into operation and, when the radiator began to conduct the heat through the steel handcuffs, it was discovered that no one had a key to fit them. The fire brigade had had to be called out to saw through them and release the overheated prisoner!

The inspector remonstrated with us but our amusement did little to placate him.

'Just shows that we caught him red-handed!'

Fortunately, Nat Sheron stepped in and got rid of him.

We had encountered resistance in making one or two of the arrests, but there had been nothing we couldn't handle. By midnight, seven burglars were behind bars and we had rooms full of recovered property. We were exhausted but we had been on a roll so the adrenaline was still pumping. By the time the last charge sheet had been typed and the last case-file completed we had effectively been on duty for almost forty hours.

The next day was equally hectic as we continued with interviews and further inquiries into the team's activities. Bell was now willing to admit all the offences he had committed and help us to recover stolen goods that he had sold on. We were out with him for several hours as he pointed out homes he had attacked, and several other homes where people lived who had received his stolen goods. There was a slight problem. Just after his release from prison he had been arrested for a theft and had failed to answer his bail at the Crown Court. So now we had to take him there as they held precedence over his immediate future but, naturally, we needed him in our custody so that he could cleanse his soul of his sins. We explained the situation to a sympathetic barrister and were eventually called into court.

I was handcuffed to Bell while the judge had the situation explained to him. He endorsed the view that it was only proper that we should be able to complete our urgent inquiries. He deemed that Bell should be bailed to the police for twenty-four hours and then handed over to the prison authorities at Walton jail the following day. He began to outline these conditions and, to my bewilderment, I realised that he was addressing his comments to the prisoner!

In fairness, Bell was clad in a smart suit that had been brought into the station for him and had also enjoyed a good night's sleep. I was unshaven, hollow-eyed and clad in sweatshirt and jeans. To some amusement, the mistake was rectified and I had to sign as surety for him.

No one had ever heard of a police officer going bail for his own prisoner before!

An inquiry that extended to six months resulted in a final tally of twenty-three arrests, twelve for burglary, the remainder for receiving stolen goods. We had also detected well over 300 attacks on dwelling houses and recovered many thousands of pounds' worth of property, which could now be returned to the grateful owners. The greed of some folk also came to light. People of excellent reputation and with good jobs had been tempted by a cheap price. One man held a responsible position in local industry but had nevertheless bought a stolen colour television. We called at his home one Saturday morning only to be told by his teenage daughter that her parents were out shopping. Without identifying ourselves, we told her we would call back later. When we did so, we were met with an explosion of indignation as we told him the purpose of our visit.

'I play golf with your boss. He will most certainly hear about this!'

He was insistent that he only possessed the black and white television that was in the lounge. He demanded that we look at it and, having done so, Mike rubbed his chin.

'Yes, sir, our boss certainly will hear about this. Just as soon as you tell us where the colour television set is that we saw through the window an hour ago!'

He took us to his sister's home in an adjacent road. Having guessed who his visitors were, he had dashed around to conceal it. She got nicked, as well, so that was some favour he did her.

A week or so later we arrested a barmaid from a local pub for buying a stolen diamond ring. We picked her up in the city centre and dealt with her at St Anne's Street station. After we had charged her, she rang the licencee of the pub to collect her and drive her home. We were talking to her when the phone rang. A constable on the front desk informed us that the licencee had arrived. Mike made his way down the stairs and, as he did so, he suddenly remembered a snippet of information we had been given by one of the prisoners. This licencee was supposed to have bought a very expensive cigarette-lighter stolen from one of the houses. When he arrived in the foyer he saw that this licencee was smoking. Drawing his own packet from his pocket, Mike identified himself and asked for a light for his cigarette.

'Er, I'm sorry, I don't have a light on me.'

'How did you light yours?'

'The officer on the desk gave me a light.'

'D'you really want me to waste my time and speak to him? If I have to, I will waste yours, pal.'

Mike held his hand out and, after a little hesitation, the gold lighter was placed in his palm. One more for the cells, boss.

The Scouse humour shows through whatever the circumstances. We pulled one lad from his bed early one morning and nicked him. Taking him to Speke Police Station, Mike brought him before the custody sergeant, Jim Hall. Mike outlined the circumstances of his arrest and requested that he be detained while we continued our inquiries. Jim began to take his details for the charge sheet.

'Name, lad?'

'Gerald Arthur Reid, Sarge.'

'Date of birth?'

'Twelfth of December, 1952.'

'What is your occupation?'

'Retired robber, Sarge.'

Jim peered up from the desk.

'When did you retire, lad.'

'About fifteen minutes ago when Mr Johnson put me door in!'

The gang of burglars eventually appeared before the Recorder of Liverpool, His Honour Mr Justice Lyons. They all pleaded guilty to specimen charges and had numerous offences taken into consideration. Judge Lyons was scathing in his condemnation of them.

'Within two months of release from prison sentences you once again began to prey on the public, stealing a great quantity of valuable property. The gravity of burglary is not to be measured solely by the amount of property stolen. One young woman in a house that you have admitted burgling has said that, since the burglary, she is afraid to even go upstairs in the dark. She is so frightened at night that she now has to sleep with her mother.'

He sentenced them to long prison terms and commended us for the intelligence and hard work we had put in to the inquiry.

Chapter Nine

One lunchtime Tom and I were travelling to see to see a contact in Speke. As we approached the airport we noticed a blue Vauxhall car containing three men on the opposite carriageway.

'Hang on, Tom, is that the car that was circulated on the radio a little earlier?'

A general message had recently been transmitted alerting all patrols to keep observations for this vehicle. Earlier that morning a motorist had had a row with the occupants of this car over the manner of their driving and one of them had threatened him with a handgun. Not surprisingly, the driver had conceded that he had no further argument and had sped away. He had made his way to Garston nick and reported the incident.

I pulled my car around and accelerated, catching up with the Vauxhall as we drove into Garston. We followed the car under the railway bridge as Tom made efforts to summon assistance. His radio was faulty, judging by the static that was coming from the receiver. The occupants of the car were obviously aware of our presence behind them but we could raise no back-up. From our point of view, they then did the worst thing that they could have done – they drove into a narrow street off Window Lane, which was a dead end. They stopped and I parked my car at an angle so that we had them blocked in. Muttering curses about radios and life in general, Tom thrust open his door. We both alighted and approached the Vauxhall.

'Detective Sergeant Hall. Hand me the gun. NOW!'

'What gun, boss?' replied the driver, nervously licking his lips.

'This is not a debating society. The bloody gun, NOW!'

As the rear-seat passenger began to reach under his seat I wrestled his door open and dragged him onto the pavement. I retrieved a firearm from the well of the car seat and I was mightily relieved to discover it was an imitation. Even at close quarters I would have defied anyone to tell the difference. Tommy nicked them all and we took them to Garston Police Station. They were detained to be dealt with by the officers who had attended the original incident.

We left the station and, as we were getting into our car, Tom changed his mind about going to Speke.

'That can wait till later. Let's go for a pint at the Cavalier, we deserve one.'

'OK, Tom, but why there?'

Although fairly close, his choice of pubs puzzled me. The Gay Cavalier was one rough watering hole. Certainly any such person of that name would have received short shrift had he ventured inside.

'Mike, after the shock we have just had I would hate to be the guy who crossed me.'

OK, with Tom I knew it made sense.

We never did have much luck with police radios.

Mike had just got us a rollicking regarding a conversation that he had had on air with the force control room. We were prowling the streets one night when a general message came over:

'Any mobile, observations requested for a dog which has recently escaped from a yard on the Dock Road, Garston. Described as a Dalmatian breed, over.'

'1CS 73, over,' Mike immediately responded, giving our allotted call sign.

'1CS 73 go ahead, over.'

'We are in that area. We'll keep a look-out, as yet we have not spotted it.'

'1CS 73, thank you, out.'

A few minutes later we received a request on air to call into HQ and have a chat with the duty Control Room Inspector. He was not only quicker on the uptake than his operator, he certainly did not share our sense of humour!

Sod's law saw that the very next night it would happen again. Put Mike and I in the north end of the city and we would get lost. We were driving through Bootle and listening to radio transmissions regarding the pursuit of a stolen vehicle. Even with our scant knowledge of the area we soon realised that the chase was taking place somewhere in our vicinity. With only a scream of tyres by way of warning, the stolen car passed us, having managed to evade his nearest pursuer. I took up the chase. He was driving like a maniac as we hurtled through the suburban roads at crazy speeds.

For several miles I grimly followed him, as he risked not only his, but also our lives and those of other innocent road-users. At speeds in excess of 80mph I stayed on his tail as he tried everything to shake us off. He drove through red traffic lights, down dual carriageways in the wrong direction and mounted pavements, causing pedestrians to scatter. As I concentrated solely on controlling my vehicle Mike was giving a running commentary over the radio. Naturally this was not helped by the fact we did not have the slightest idea where we were. Mike was describing us passing churches, pubs, anything that would give the listeners a clue as to where the pursuit was taking place.

Eventually, with a wailing of klaxons and blue flashing lights, we were overtaken by a marked traffic patrol. We backed off and let the professionals take over. Within minutes it was finished. The thief lost control of the car at a junction, slid into a skid and stalled the engine.

The next day Mike and I retraced the route, this time in a rather more sedate fashion. We completed our witness statements, outlining the roads we had travelled down, and handed them to the traffic officers who had made the arrest. We thought no more of the matter until some months later when we were requested to attend the Crown Court for the trial of the driver.

We gave our evidence and listened while a traffic officer was cross-examined by the defence. In answer to a question he mentioned that a recorded copy of the transmissions made during a pursuit was always retained at HQ control room. To clear up some point he was instructed to obtain the tape so it could be played in court that afternoon.

Mike and I had given our evidence in a calm and collected manner as we described events during the chase. The tape was played in a still and silent courtroom. Mike sounded like a banshee. He could be heard screaming out directions as best as he could, while warning me in the most unprofessional language of hazards ahead. Frankly, that brought home to the jury the stress and terror of being involved in such incidents. I think that did more to convict the defendant than anything.

Naturally, I have never let Mike forget it!

Chapter Ten

Late one evening Mike and I walked into the Flying Saucer pub on the Speke estate, the toughest in the area. The customers made no secret of their displeasure at the sight of us. We couldn't have cared less. We only drank there occasionally because of their attitude and to demonstrate that there were no places we were scared to visit.

Billy Lewtas was a young man we had dealt with on a number of occasions for some criminal venture or another.

'Does Billy still drink here?' Mike asked.

'I haven't seen him for a while. Why?'

'I've had him named for a job. Apparently he did a burglary down by Western Avenue. I'll have a word when I see him.'

We drove back to Speke and, as we passed along South Parade, I glanced at a number of men leaving a fish and chip shop.

'Mike, there he is. Lewtas.'

We stopped and Mike arrested Lewtas after we had waved away the drunken protests of his companions. We took him to Speke station and had just placed him in the cell complex when we heard yelling coming from the direction of the enquiry desk. We could hear our names being shouted so we walked through to see what the commotion was about.

Another familiar face greeted us. Derek Harlow was Billy's mate and we also knew him well from previous dealings. On seeing us, he lost interest in the desk constable.

'Why have you locked Billy up?'

'Burglary, but what's it to you?'

'He didn't do it. You've got the wrong man.'

'Who says?'

'I do. It was me who screwed the chemist's on the Parade last week. I was on me own when I did it.'

'Why should we believe you?'

''Cos I've got all the gear from the job in me 'ouse.'

'Show us then.'

We drove him to his flat a mile or so from the station. This was the toughest part of the estate and, over the years, Mike and I had fought many battles there while making arrests. It was a place I was never fond of visiting at night – a quadrangle of menacing, gloomy three-storey flats. When they had been originally constructed a large tree-lined grassed area had been the centrepiece of the complex as a playground for children. Now it was rutted and strewn with rubble, rubbish and scrapped cars. All that remained of the trees were stark stumps and most of the street lighting had been smashed long ago. In early light it often reminded me of the battlefield scenes from the First World War. Mike always said that the trees hadn't been vandalised, they'd died from shame!

Derek's flat was an abomination. The conditions that

76

some people seemed content to live in sometimes astounded me. The first thing I noticed when we entered was the sickening stench.

'OK, Derek, where's the gear?' Mike was obviously as keen as I was to get out of there.

'In the bathroom, Mr Johnson.'

We entered the small room and I was disgusted at the appalling sight that greeted us. The toilet flush had obviously been broken for some time and the bowl was full to the brim with excreta. We looked about the room but there was no sign of the watches and perfume that had been stolen.

'Come on, Derek, stop playing games.'

'It's wrapped in plastic in the bog.'

'Under all that shit!'

'Yeah, good hiding place, isn't it? How are you gonna get it out, Mr Johnson?'

Mike looked at him quizzically with his head on one side.

'Now don't be silly. The question is, Derek, how are YOU going to get it out?'

Having made him remove the packages and clean them, we took him back to the station. Bristling with self-righteous indignation, he made a written statement admitting the crime. As Mike was about to charge him, Derek seemed content with his lot.

'Gotta let Billy go now, right Mr Johnson?'

'Wrong.'

'What d'you mean? I told you I did the chemist's and you've got the gear back.'

'Because,' Mike gently replied, 'we nicked Billy for screwing houses. We knew nothing about the chemists!'

Derek left the station a sadder but wiser man.

In the early hours of the morning the steward of a club in Woolton was securing the premises when he was attacked by three masked men. He was savagely beaten and tied up. The offenders stole the evening's takings and a large quantity of spirits. Mike and I were contacted by Dawn, one of our informants, a couple of days later. She had been working for us for some months and was always very reliable. She told us that one of the three robbers was a man we had dealt with before, John Every. During the conversation she made a reference to him having also done a job at a garage in Anfield Road. She had heard that this crime had been carried out some months earlier. Other than that, she was unable to give us any specific details of the matter. This was in another division on the far side of the city, so neither Mike nor I had any knowledge of the alleged incident.

Early the following morning we pulled Every from his bed at his flat in Speke. A search of his home revealed nothing of interest to us and within the hour we were interviewing him at the station. He flatly denied any knowledge of the robbery. By now we were aware that we were getting nowhere fast. The injured man was unable to identify his attackers and there was no forensic evidence to connect our suspect to the scene. However, I was reluctant to give it up, as Dawn was normally solid in what she told us. As we were running out of options I tried one last thing.

'OK, so what about the garage job in Anfield Road?'

'Fair enough, I'll put me hands up to that one.'

Just as I was beginning to think our day hadn't been wasted his eyes suddenly narrowed.

'Hang on, it may be a different one. How big is the garage you're talking about?'

We were so near but I had no answer for him. Mike thought faster than I did. Holding out his hands he gestured with them.

'You know, about so big. Pretty normal, I suppose.'

'OK, that must be the one.'

With an inward sigh of relief I settled back as Mike began to write the statement that Every dictated. Obviously we were expecting him to admit to a burglary. After he had signed the caution his first words stunned us.

'We got there just after midnight. We were in a stolen motor and parked up. We put the masks on and went in and grabbed hold of the man on the till.'

To our utter amazement he went on to admit a serious robbery. Some nine months earlier, at 4 a.m., the night attendant at this garage had been attacked. He had been forced to open the safe and a large amount of cash was stolen. Every admitted taking part in the attack and named his accomplice. He, too, was later arrested and eventually both received terms of imprisonment.

We had been lucky though – Mike's swift reaction had saved the day.

Chapter Eleven

A nasty spate of robberies had been carried out in the city centre over recent weeks. The victims, mostly youngsters, had been attacked as they took the takings from shops to the bank. It was obvious that the robbers had been observing the regular trips of staff sent to deposit considerable amounts of cash. Several young people would be emotionally scarred for life as a result of their experiences at the hands of these thugs.

Although it was not our division we were aware of the incidents, and eventually Allison, one of our informants, learnt who was responsible for the attacks. She passed their details on to us which resulted in our arresting three men in connection with these assaults. I use the word 'men' loosely in this context – it's very easy to attack vulnerable young women when you are mob-handed. When we took them out they gave us no resistance and within a week we had the team in custody.

A few days later Ken Anderson called us into his office. At first, looking at the frown on his face, I thought we were in for a rollicking but an even more unpleasant surprise was awaiting us.

'That team you have just pulled in for the robberies – have you any idea who they work for?'

'No sir, why?' Mike asked.

'The Criminal Intelligence Section have just been on to the Deputy Chief Constable Mr Dalzell. They have information from a reliable source that they are part of Harry Crawshaw's team.'

Crawshaw was a criminal with a pedigree background and, without doubt, one of the major gangsters on the Liverpool scene with contacts country wide. He maintained the façade of a successful businessman but no one was in any doubt what his true role was. Crawshaw was a premier-league thug and his team were feared by most on the criminal scene. He was not a man to cross lightly.

'So we've rattled Crawshaw's cage; what's wrong with that?'

'As yet we don't know. They have word that he has put a contract out on you.'

'A contract?' I asked, somewhat bemused.

'Yes, he wants to have you badly beaten up. He's looking to have you put in hospital. He's determined to settle the score but we don't know what's so particular about this job to upset him.'

'What the hell are we supposed to do?' Mike responded.

'I don't like having to tell you this, and we doubt that even Crawshaw is stupid enough to go this far, but an anonymous telephone came in this morning saying that you're going to be shot. Mr Dalzell suggests you may be better moving to another division.'

I looked at Mike who gave a slight shake of his head before I responded. 'There's little point in that. It will be months before these cases come up at the Crown Court and, if they want us, they can always find us. It could be any nutter who made that call. Leave it to us, we'll watch our backs.'

'Mr Dalzell is adamant that you do nothing about this information. The Intelligence Section are conducting an investigation and it must be left to them. He also instructs that you both carry a personal radio, on and off duty.'

Saying this, he handed us two radios. 'Now, get my meaning straight. You do not get involved, understand?'

Giving him the assurances that he wanted, we left his office. Mike and I talked the situation over and agreed that, as it stood, there was little we could do. The next thing I did was to toss the radio into my desk drawer. As I lived on the Wirral I was far out of transmission range should an incident occur. Within a few days the matter had gone to the back of our minds. We had tried to contact our informant but she was nowhere to be found.

Mike and I were trained surveillance officers and I automatically practised anti-surveillance tactics on my travels. Just after six one evening, I left a crowded Mersey Tunnel and joined the speeding traffic on the congested M53 motorway. As I had been paying my toll at the booth I had become aware of a red Cortina with three men aboard behind me. Despite the heavy traffic, I noticed this car keeping pace with me as I weaved in and out of the lanes. I made a note of the registration number and waited until the last possible second as we approached my exit junction. I crossed from the outer lane at such a speed the Cortina had no chance of making a similar manoeuvre and it carried on, trapped in the traffic flow.

I smiled to myself that I was probably overreacting as I drove onto my estate. Stopping at the shops, I bought an evening paper and paused to chat with Sheila and Mike Dickin who were neighbours and friends. As we talked, the Cortina entered the estate and drove past us and out of sight. None of the occupants noticed me, they never glanced in our direction. They must have come off at the next junction which was a mile or so along the motorway.

I rang Mike at home to tell him about this development and we decided to keep it to ourselves. If we had told Ken he would in all probability have grounded us behind our desks. I checked the vehicle registration number and was informed that at present there was no registered owner of this vehicle. A couple of days later Mike spotted the same car tailing him on his way home but he easily lost it in the traffic chaos around the Childwall Fiveways junction. Talking it over the following day, neither of us were happy.

'What do you reckon?' Mike asked me.

'OK, have a go at us, but not our families.'

'If they're trying to find out where we live, they're serious.'

'We've been told to stay out of it, remember.'

'Yeah, leave it to the Intelligence Section, right?'

'Who can only act when something's happened.'

The Intelligence Section was exactly what the title suggested. A group of officers who were engaged only in compiling information relating to major crime figures. They were not involved in any specific inquiries and rarely made arrests, so neither of us were too impressed.

'I'm not happy about this now.'

'Neither am I. I don't like things being out of our control.'

'We need to know more about why we are targets.'

'Yeah, let's find Allison and see what else she knows.'

'I say we have a go at the bastards. Let's take it to them first.'

'I'll go along with that. But we had better get the message across when we do. When Ken finds out he'll hit the roof.'

'Why should you worry? You'll probably blame me as usual.'

The first thing was to find our contact but we hit a stumbling block. Allison was not at her usual haunts and we had no permanent address for her. A couple of days later one of the girls told us that she was staying out of the way, working over the water in Birkenhead. That night Mike and I cruised around the gloomy red-light district of the dock, just outside the town centre. After an hour we found her leaving a ship where she had been entertaining the crew.

She was nervous on seeing us but filled us in on the entire picture when we took her to the Duke pub in Corporation Road, one favoured by the street girls. She told us that Crawshaw had gone insane over the arrests. He was blazing, incandescent and, from what she told us, we now knew why – one of the men we had arrested was his nephew! We had had no idea of this as it was not entered in any of his criminal record files. Crawshaw was treating it as personal insult that we had had the temerity to arrest a relative and he had ordered revenge. If we could not be taken out, then our families were to be attacked as they would be a far softer option. He was also leaving no stone unturned to discover the identity of the informant who had been helping us.

We promised to look after a very shaken Allison, who had become embroiled in something that seemed to be escalating out of control. If necessary we would have her moved to another address. This brought her some relief as she already knew we would never divulge her identity. In the hard life on the streets she had to trust us. If not her life, she had certainly placed her health in our hands. We dropped her off to continue her trade, having given her some cash, and we returned to Liverpool in silence. Over a drink in the Pink Parrot club in Duke Street we considered our options. Mike was positive in his view.

'That's it. I am definitely going to face him down. No one, and I mean no one, is getting anywhere near my family.'

'Yeah, what's the worst that can happen? At least he'll know where we're coming from. He's gone over the limit now. I'm not trusting this to anyone else.'

After further discussion we came up with a plan of action for the following day and we parted for the night. On my way home I kept a constant watch in my rear-view mirror. The next day we drove around Toxteth and, just after noon, we spotted a Jaguar car outside a pub in Wavertree. We knew it belonged to Crawshaw and parked up. At the time this pub was frequented by the hard men on the crime scene and when we entered we discovered that the place was packed. Crawshaw was sitting at a corner table holding court with a group of cronies. He probably knew we were coming in before he saw us.

'Mr Mulloy, Mr Johnson, how nice to see you. John, get the lads a drink – scotch isn't it?'

Without replying to his greeting we sat at the table and looked directly into his eyes. Over six foot tall, heavily built with short cropped hair, he was immaculately dressed and sported expensive jewellery; His group consisted of several burly younger men all dressed in dark suits. They sat stiffly, surveying us with unsmiling faces and narrowed eyes. I could feel the tension rising as they awaited developments. Nothing was said for a few minutes until the drinks were placed in front of us. I broke the menacing silence.

'Harry, word has it you're being a bad boy.'

'You know me, Mr Mulloy. That's all behind me. I'm legit now, in business.'

'Yeah, so are we in business. Bad business. Especially for you. If you start a war you never know who might get hurt.'

'Are you threatening me?'

'Let's say we're pointing out the facts of life. You come for us, we can understand that. Make it personal with our families and the gloves are off and we'll deal with you. No one else. Just you! You'd better understand, you are right out of order. We won't be coming as the law. Just as ourselves and that means no control whatsoever! I definitely would not recommend it as being good for your health.'

As I delivered this message to him I saw a flicker of doubt enter his eyes.

'You two are as bloody mad as they say you are. You come on to my patch and threaten me! I'm gonna see Rexie about this.'

Rexie Makin was the most prominent solicitor in Liverpool and we had crossed swords with him on numerous occasions. We had respect for him as a fair but challenging advocate.

Mike laughed. 'Rexie! How often do you see him in his Rolls Royce driving round here?'

'Never, why?'

'But you see Mr Mulloy and I every day. Think about it, Harry. Every day! Until we hear that you've got our message we'll keep an eye on your house and family when we're passing. We already know where you live, right?'

As we stood up to leave, Mike picked up the two untouched glasses of whisky. He upturned them on to the table and the contents poured out. In the ominous silence which enveloped the entire pub, the drip of the spilt drink seemed inordinately loud. Crawshaw glared at us with malevolent hatred on his face. Without a further word we made our way out.

The next morning we were again summoned to Ken's office. He came directly to the point.

'What the hell were you doing in Wavertree?'

'When boss?' Mike asked with an innocent air.

'Don't bloody when me! Yesterday, that's when.'

'Oh, yes, that's right. Just called in to a local pub for a drink, why?'

'I suppose it was mere coincidence that Crawshaw just happened to be there?'

'Now that you mention it, he was. In fact we had a little chat with him about things in general.'

'Well, the little chat has him convinced that you two are mental cases. I thought I told you to stay out of it.'

'Boss, we just pointed out that it could end up in his own back yard.'

We got a dressing down, but it was worth it. Ken was always very supportive and totally loyal to his staff and his heart was not in it. He informed us that Crawshaw had dropped any thoughts of revenge as he feared the backlash from us. If he had had any doubts he was now only too aware that there was no way we would have allowed the threats to have ended up on our doorsteps. Our families had enough to put up with. That was something we would never have tolerated in any circumstances.

Chapter Twelve

Mike and I were reaching the end of a hard day. We had just finished at the Crown Court at the conclusion of a lengthy trial of several burglars. We had spent three weeks there, most of the time being insulted and threatened by various members of their families and friends. We had been accused of 'fitting them up', by fabricating evidence against them. They had been found guilty and received lengthy prison sentences. Leaving the building, their friends had been even more angry because of the result but we had just shrugged the tirade off.

Now it was late evening and we had just completed the case reports and they were ready for filing. Mike stretched and yawned.

'I've had enough. Fancy a pint?'

He twisted my arm so I agreed to his proposal. We decided to go to the Shakespeare club in the city centre where, apart from a drink, we could view the act. It was late when we eventually got there and the cabaret was in progress. Through the gloom we made our way to the bar on the upper floor. Collecting our drinks, we watched the singer until he eventually reached the end of his spot and the lights came back on.

'I don't believe it!'

I glanced over my shoulder to see what Mike meant and my heart sank. Sitting at several tables close by were the friends and relatives of the men who had been sent down earlier that day. A young woman rose to her feet and approached us.

Although she was very attractive she had been the worst of all them over the days at the Crown Court. She stood in front of us with her hands on her hips.

'Mr Mulloy, Mr Johnson. How nice to see you again.'

'Look, there's no point in trouble, Kim. If it starts we may lose, but just remember we know who you all are!'

'Mr Mulloy, we don't want any grief. We're having a few drinks to drown our sorrows. D'you want to have a drink with us?'

'Hang on, Kim,' Mike interrupted, 'you in particular have spent the last three weeks trying to make our lives a misery. Now you're asking us to the family party. What's the score?'

'Come on, you know what it is. The lads were bang at it and you nicked them fair and square. But you've got to do your piece for them and make a show, know what I mean?'

Somewhat incredulously we did join them. Not only did we spend rather a pleasant hour in their company, that young woman went on to become a very reliable informant for us from that time on.

Like most police officers I often got frustrated with the judicial system. Although, technically, my part ended in putting someone before the courts, often the sentences made a mockery of the victim's suffering. Sometimes, though, the penalty resulting from an offence was far more than anyone should have been expected to pay.

I was with Tom one morning when an urgent radio call caused us to rush to a premises in the Dingle. We found the very shaken manager of the shop being comforted by a female uniformed officer who had been the first to attend the scene. She told us briefly what to expect and we made our way through the premises. The back door of the shop had been forced open and was swinging from the hinges. A lorry was parked in the rear yard and we could see that it had been loaded up, presumably with stock from the shop. That was not the reason for our urgent attendance. The bonnet of the lorry was up against the sturdy yard gates and crushed in the middle was a dead body!

We both knew him. Gerry was a prolific burglar and we had dealt with him on a number of occasions. What fascinated me was that in his right hand he held a cigarette. The ash had burnt down to the filter tip but remained intact. As I looked into his open, sightless eyes I recognised that he had paid the ultimate price for this crime.

It was a simple enough inquiry to complete. He had broken into the shop and had intended to use the lorry to remove his haul. He had managed to get it started and had then gone to open the rear gates. Unfortunately, he must have left the handbrake off and the heavy vehicle had trundled down the slight incline. Caught unawares, he was crushed to death. We later attended the post-mortem which verified our conclusions.

*

Often I met people in adversity who showed such courage that I felt nothing but admiration for them. Margaret was a twenty-year-old student at Liverpool university. Her home was in Wales so she shared a flat with other students in Devonshire Road. This area of Toxteth was very popular with students and they were dotted all over the place. In the early hours of the morning she had left one such flat and was walking the short distance back to her own home. As she passed some bushes a man leapt out at her.

Grabbing her by the throat, he dragged her into the undergrowth and her terrible ordeal began. Pressing a knife to her throat, he demanded she strip off her clothes. Over the next hour he raped her and forced her to perform perverse sexual acts. Only as dawn was breaking did her nightmare come to an end. She was so terrified she did not even bother to dress. In fear that he would return to continue his molestation, she ran to raise the alarm with her flatmates with her clothing draped around her.

I took the inquiry on and from the outset I was impressed by her. She was determined that she would put this behind her and not let it destroy her future. She had been convinced that her attacker was going to kill her after he had finished with her sexually. Fearing for her life, she had pretended she had been enjoying the sexual activity and was attracted to him. She had got him talking and, incredibly, had made a date with him!

A medical examination confirmed her allegations. Other officers who knew of the appointment she had made with the rapist were sceptical of him appearing, but I believed there was a good chance that he would.

She was a very level-headed girl and also extremely attractive. If she had actually managed to persuade him that she did fancy him, he may not have been able to avoid the temptation of enjoying her favours again.

The following night I sat near to her in the lounge of the Philharmonic pub on the fringe of the city centre. The pub was thronged with students from the nearby university and nobody took any notice of Tom and Mike sitting at a table by the door. Suddenly she stiffened and indicated to me with her eyes a man who had just entered. As he was peering about I nodded to the lads who had been watching me intently. We waited until he approached her. As she shrank back in revulsion he realised something was amiss and turned to leave.

Too late.

He admitted everything and his victim at least had the satisfaction of seeing him go to prison for many years.

For nearly two months Mike and I had been working undercover in the Manchester area on a drugs case. We had been seconded there as part of a major operation to infiltrate a gang who were putting huge quantities of amphetamines on to the streets of several cities. The local informant had introduced us as armed robbers from Liverpool. Our cover story was that we were interested in putting our stolen cash into drugs. The team we were looking at were so professional that for our safety no chances were being taken. We were also made fully aware that they had a background of unbridled violence.

It was a stressful time as we were dealing with dangerous and volatile characters and we had to be constantly looking over our shoulders. We held numerous meetings with the team over the weeks in Manchester and we both felt very vulnerable. It had been decided that these discussions would be held in public places, such as the bars at various hotels around Piccadilly in the city centre. On the first occasion we had other officers posing as customers to cover our backs. That was the only time we had that luxury. The team were so surveillance conscious there was a real fear that the operation would be in jeopardy. From then on, Mike and I agreed to go it alone – not happily I must add. We could not even carry a warrant card for fear we may have been searched. On the first few of these gatherings we were invited into the toilets and inspected, so as to satisfy them that we were not wearing taping equipment.

As the weeks passed these men relaxed with us somewhat. Eventually we managed to gather a lot of intelligence regarding their organisation. As this was passed on to the Manchester officers they began to complete the whole picture. Eventually, from names they mentioned and details that came to light, it was enough to identify the entire infrastructure of the gang and, most importantly, the location of the premises where they were manufacturing and storing the amphetamines. The day before we were expected to meet to finalise the purchase of drugs, search warrants were executed in Manchester and Wigan. All the key figures were arrested and a large quantity of drugs and cash recovered. Mike and I took no part in that activity, we simply vanished back into the shadows from where we had come.

I was glad it was over but there was a humorous side to the operation. On one occasion we were invited to a party at the impressive home of one of the dealers at Bramhall in Cheshire, a very desirable residential area. The Manchester officers were interested as to who may be there, so we accepted the offer.

The house was crowded and there were a number of young women present. As Mike was getting us a drink, Peter, our host came over to me. He mentioned that if Mike or I wanted a woman for the night to let him know. Several of these girls were apparently high-class prostitutes he had hired for the occasion. When Mike returned clutching our drinks, I mentioned this to him. There was absolutely no way we could have got involved with any of them. In the future we would be in the witness box giving evidence and such behaviour would have been wonderful ammunition against us. There was also the wrath of Carol and Sylvia to consider!

'What did you say to him?' Mike asked.

'First thing that came into my head.'

'Better tell me, so that our stories agree.'

'I said you were gay.'

'YOU SAID WHAT?' was Mike's strangled response.

'I had to think on my feet, just forget about it.'

'Forget about it! You never told him you were bloody gay! I'll never forgive you for this! Don't you ever tell anyone about it!'

I tried my best to keep a straight face.

'I think that could be the least of your problems,' I told him.

He eyed me suspiciously. 'Why?'

'I think he's gone to find you a fella!'

Chapter Thirteen

Driving through the city centre one day, we responded to a 'robbery in progress' call on the radio. Three men had entered a furrier's shop in Bold Street, attacked the two female staff who had tried to stop them and had escaped with arm-loads of jackets from the racks. We drove down the back streets and spotted them almost immediately. They ran off as we approached in the car and began throwing the stolen coats away. We quickly got jammed in the traffic flow so I alighted and continued the pursuit on foot. Mike did his best to force the police car through the traffic and also collect the discarded coats.

They were still ahead of me but I was gaining when they turned the corner into Wostenholme Square. There was absolutely no sight of them when I made the junction. I was joined by my partner and we tried to work out where they could have gone. A new club was being fitted out and we entered to find it buzzing with workmen. In response to our enquiries they denied anyone had entered the building. We were just about to leave when the foreman came in. By a remarkable coincidence he was my next-door neighbour, and in response to his greeting I explained why I was there.

'Hitting women! Bastards never told us that!'

The workmen who had been listening strode over to a heap of planks and brawny arms dragged the three culprits out from under them! They had been willing to give anyone a break, but not for attacking women.

There is no doubt that the success of a detective relies mainly on his sources of information. Although people inform for many reasons, such as money or revenge, it is a vital tool of a detective's trade – especially when a rapport grows between you and your informant, based on past experience and trust. Months of work can be short-circuited by the conduit of criminal intelligence.

Mike and I were chatting to one such contact when he mentioned two young men who he said were on the run and wondered if we were interested. What he said next ensured we were all ears. The men had been wanted for over two years! They had to be bang at crime. He told us that they were always flush with money and boasting of jobs they had committed. He gave us an address in the Huyton area and the following morning we gave them a call just after six. We took another couple of lads with us, which turned out to be just as well. We searched the house, and although we were not welcomed by the occupants, it was accepted as a fact of life. There was no sign of the men but our contact had told us they had boasted of hiding during previous searches. We checked again and found that they were concealed in a cupboard under the stairs.

Immediately all hell broke loose. They were manic in their efforts to resist arrest and all the family, complete with kids and the Alsatian dog, joined in. We were being struck with implements, bitten, kicked and punched. In the mêlée we had no idea who was responsible. In a cursing, struggling mass we fell into the kitchen. One of the youths grabbed hold of a kitchen knife and was trying his best to stab us. Eventually we overpowered them and amazingly, other than scrapes and bruises, no one was badly hurt.

After they had calmed down, our interviews resulted in them admitting a long catalogue of house burglaries and numerous robberies. They had targeted homosexuals in various parts of the city as vulnerable victims. In all it was a good result, two dangerous men off the streets and well over 200 jobs cleared up in several police areas. It shows you could never tell what you were up against.

In a case where so many offences are committed it is normal to charge the more serious ones and list the others to be taken into consideration by the court. It is required that the victims in such cases are notified and give their consent for the procedure. When the matter was finally resolved, one CID boss had nearly a hundred detections on his patch. Having received the file, he instructed a sergeant to attend personally to all the complainants to check that I had notified them! Not only was it waste of time, what on earth was he hoping to achieve? From then on, he was a man I was very short with.

One morning when I had come back from court, I entered the general office to find Tom in a deep discussion with Mike. They brought me up to date on a job that was going down at lunchtime. They had received information that a gang from Garston intended to rob the female owner of a small betting shop on the Speke estate. She was in the habit of going to the bank each afternoon with her early takings and the team had been watching her daily routine. Now the job was coming off. Tom looked at me for a moment before turning to Mike.

'He'd do, wouldn't he?'

Mike agreed with him so rapidly that my suspicions were immediately aroused.

'Do for what?'

'Take her place and use her car.'

'No way, forget it!'

'Come on, you don't have to wear a frock.'

'No?'

'No, just her long coat and a wig. She normally wears trousers, anyway.'

'That's all?'

'Honestly. Oh, and a bit of make-up!'

Eventually they talked me into it, against my better judgement. The plan was that I would travel to the shop and liaise with the owner, who was fully aware of the situation. At the appropriate time I would leave the shop, clad in her coat and a wig, and make my way to her car, openly carrying her briefcase. This meant I would be in the open for the length of time it would take to cover the fifty yards to where her car was parked. This was the danger zone. My two companions would be in an unmarked observation van on the forecourt and marked police cars would also be in close proximity, but out of sight.

An hour before the attack was expected I was dropped off at the shop. I got myself ready and before I closed the briefcase I put in two housebricks that I had brought with me. Eventually, with a dry mouth, I opened the door and began to make my way to her car. Although I was aware that the attack could come at any time I forced myself to stroll and not look about. Out of the corner of my eye I had already noticed two men in the pub doorway watching me. On the forecourt was a white Cortina car with another man in the driving seat and he had the engine running. This was definitely going to come down.

It was over within a minute. I heard running footsteps behind me and I waited until the last second before I whirled around. Two burly men with stocking masks were rushing straight at me, both armed with baseball bats. I heard my companions crashing out of the van, and as the first assailant got to me I hit him in the face with the briefcase and he went down as if he had been shot. His companion hesitated and the lads were all over him. The getaway driver abandoned his mates, but only got a few hundred yards before he was hemmed in by police cars and arrested. They were all handcuffed and Tom arrested them for conspiracy to rob. As we were getting our breath back Mike looked at me with a mischievous grin.

'Come on Mike, give us a kiss!'

He was fortunate that I was no longer in possession of the briefcase.

Tommy was dealing with a job where the offender responsible had been eluding him for some months. The man had become involved in an argument with the staff at a pub and had been ejected. An hour or so later he returned armed with a sawn-off shotgun. Just like the Wild West, this cowboy blew away the optics and part of the bar and then escaped into the night. Despite Tom's best efforts to track him down he vanished. I had a man in custody who was looking for favours and he 'threw up' an address in the Kensington area where he could be found. I rang Tom and we arranged to meet later that night in the Grapes pub in the city centre, famous for its connection with the Beatles. We decided to hit the address just after dawn.

The following daybreak we took the flat out and arrested the suspect and also recovered a handgun. We caught him in bed with a nubile young brunette and this hard man of Liverpool was distraught. OK, we had him for serious firearm offences. That was the least of his worries. At the flat he confided to Tom what his real concern was. He was married, and if his wife found out the circumstances of his arrest, he would be terrified ever to sleep alongside her again. He was so affected he was clutching his private parts as he spoke! Tom had a little smile on his lips and a twinkle in his eye. This one should not give him too much trouble under the circumstances.

Bryn and Joy Owen were friends of Carol and I from our teenage days. They had emigrated to British Columbia and we were delighted when they came home on a visit to see their families. We were enjoying a drink with them one evening in the Fox and Hounds in Barnston on the Wirral when an off-duty uniformed dog-handler came in. He gave me an embarrassed greeting before shuffling off to join his company. It was little wonder that he was anxious to distance himself from me.

The previous evening Mike and I had taken a prisoner into Garston nick and this officer had brought in a drunken whining prisoner for shop-breaking. He asked the desk sergeant if he could leave him as he had an urgent matter to attend to. He could not have picked a worse man to ask, Sergeant Hindley was one of the real old school.

'No, you brought him in, you stay here!' he snapped.

'But, Sarge, you don't understand. I've got to look for me dog.'

To an audience that listened with widening grins he explained his predicament. His hound was a new one and out on his first patrol. As they had been standing in Garston village, the drunk had smashed a shop window and begun to loot the display. He had been promptly arrested in full view of a long bus queue. That was where the dog-handler's problems began. The mutt got completely carried away by the first real action he had encountered and had decided to mark his first arrest with his fangs. His handler now found himself in a quandary. In one hand he held the dog on a leash trying to bite the prisoner. In the other he held a man trying to put as much distance as possible between himself and the flashing teeth. It certainly did not help that he was being watched by an intrigued crowd. Eventually the dog got so frustrated that it bit the first thing it could reach. Unfortunately they just happened to be his handler's testicles!

Yelping in pain, with tears in his eyes and clutching the offended parts, the handler temporally lost interest in the proceedings. He released the leash and the dog promptly ran off. He was left with his prisoner who made an impassioned plea.

'Please, boss, don't blame me for bitin' yer there!'

The sergeant was not impressed at all and a general call was put out for the missing hound. Half an hour later the doors of the station crashed open and we could hear officers fighting with an obviously violent prisoner. As we went to help, four burly constables fell in carrying a fighting-mad police dog dangling upside down. The mutt had to be placed in a cell to calm down for an hour or so!

Chapter Fourteen

At 5.30 on a bright August evening the 69-year-old proprietor of a betting shop in the Dingle area left his premises and walked the short distance to his car. Before he could reach it, he was approached by three men. Without warning he was punched in the face and kicked to the ground. He was threatened with a handgun and his briefcase containing the day's taking was wrenched from him. He was left badly shaken, bruised and battered. It was a nasty assault on an elderly man who was unable to defend himself. Several weeks passed and we were no further to knowing who was responsible for the attack.

Late one evening I was with Mike in the Pineapple in Park Road. John, one of my best informants, entered and, as he ordered his drink, he nodded in the direction of the back room. We finished our conversation with the publican and followed him through.

'Heard I'd find you here, Mr Mulloy. How are you, Mr Johnson?'

'I'm fine, John,' Mike responded.

'Look, gents, that robbery of the bookie. I know who was carrying the shooter on it.'

'Who was it?'

'John Lomax. D'you know him?'

'Yeah, big guy, mid-twenties, lives in Warwick Gardens.'

'Used to live there. He's keeping out of the way, getting his head down anywhere he can.'

'Who was he with?'

'No idea. He was drunk and boasting about the job last night in a club in town. He's dyed his hair blond by the way.'

'Any idea where we can find him, John?'

'Yeah, I do as a matter of fact. D'you know the blonde stripper from the Gladray club?'

'Who doesn't know her? I've seen Bella naked more times than my own wife!'

'Well, he's seeing her in the Oslo club tonight, about midnight.'

I bought John a drink and we chatted about other matters. After he left, we began to make our plans for Lomax. He was a bad man in drink, with a reputation for instant violence. The Oslo club, just outside the city centre, was little more than a drinking den, patronised by clients who had little time for the authorities. Although we could not choose the venue, at least we knew where we stood. Just after midnight we walked into the club foyer to be greeted by scarcely masked hostility from the head doorman and his colleagues.

'Are you members?'

'Don't be a cheeky bastard, if you know what's good for you. You know who we are.'

'Only members can come in here, Mr Mulloy.'

'How can I put this so you will understand. First of all Mr Johnson and I are coming in. Secondly, none of you are going into the main lounge before us. Thirdly, any trouble from you and you will find your arse in a cell within minutes. Is that clear enough for you!'

After a minute or so spent staring at me in a futile attempt at intimidation, he backed down and stood aside. We entered the club and found it to be thronged with customers. A band was about to begin their act on the stage and we separated to see if we could see Lomax or Bella. We also kept a constant watch on each other. We were under no illusion that we were unwelcome intruders and could expect no help if all hell broke out. I had already seen several customers we had arrested who would only be too willing to extract revenge if the opportunity arose.

Mike suddenly gestured to me to join him. Sitting at a table right by the stage was our target. To say that his hair was now blond was an understatement. It was so bright and so badly done that, rather than disguise him, it drew attention to him. The group had just started to perform and, as we pushed through the milling crowd, Bella spotted us and muttered something to Lomax. After a hasty glance in our direction he immediately leapt onto the stage and to the band's amazement pretended to be part of the act. His efforts resulted in a torrent of abuse and foul language from the audience and the band broke down in confusion. As an attempt to fool us it was as much an unmitigated disaster as his hair! By this time we were at the stage and I beckoned him to join us. He did so and was obviously not intending to cause any trouble.

'You know me – DS Mulloy. We're arresting you for armed robbery.'

'OK, boss.'

'Tell you what, John,' Mike added, 'stick to robbery for a living, you're a lousy singer!'

We took him to Lark Lane nick and he eventually made a written statement of admission concerning his part in the robbery. He emphatically refused to name his accomplices and we never did trace them. Some months later he appeared at Liverpool Crown Court for trial, and by now had obviously had time to reconsider his situation while in custody. He entered a not guilty plea to the robbery charge and the case went for trial. From the outset it was patently obvious that the defence tactic was to attack our evidence. It was strongly put to us that Lomax had never dictated any statement to us. He denied signing the three-page confession and initialling the numerous minor errors. He also completely refuted the endorsement at the end which stated that he had read and agreed with the contents. We faced a lengthy and belligerent examination in which we were accused of malpractice in the compilation of this statement. It is difficult to defend yourself against such allegations. Other than to insist that the correct procedures have been complied with, there is little you can do.

When Lomax entered the witness box he went further and told the court that it would have been impossible for him to have read and checked the statement as he was completely illiterate. He could not be shaken from this and his barrister, the late Ian Stanley, then called his mother to give evidence on her son's behalf. Not for one minute could he have anticipated what was about to occur. Having gone over the family background and her relationship with her lovely lad, he reached the crux of the matter.

'Now, Mrs Lomax, it is correct, is it not, that John can neither read nor write?'

'You mean my John?'

'Yes. I am given to understand that he can do neither.'

'Who do you think you are? Saying things like that! Of course he can read and write! He's dead bright, always was at school. Saying thinks like that about my John, indeed! How dare you?'

Poor Ian looked demented, as if he was about to tear his wig off in frustration. His star witness had just blown his case out of court. Mum stood in the witness box bristling with self-righteous indignation about such a slur on her son. Something had gone badly wrong with the game plan. Ian knew better than to continue and hastily commented that he had no further questions. And Arthur Noble, the barrister for the Crown, knew better that to cross-examine her. After all, Ian had just done his job for him!

Not surprisingly, Lomax was found guilty by the jury. Before sentencing, Judge Davies commented: 'This was a bare-faced and planned robbery. This is precisely the sort of offence which has become so prevalent through-out the country, and particularly in Liverpool, over the last few years.'

He then sentenced Lomax to prison. Somehow Mrs Lomax still hadn't got the message. As Mike and I left the court she approached us.

'Bastards, telling lies about my John. I'll get you for this.'

'Norma, accept it, love, he did that robbery.'

'I know that, I'm not talking about robbin'. Saying he

can't read or write. I'll bloody swing for you one day, Mulloy!'

Having finished her tirade, she stormed off. Mike turned to me with a wry smile.

'What's it like being so popular?'

'How d'you mean?'

'Not many coppers have people prepared to commit suicide for them!'

Despite almost daily confrontations over the years, I enjoyed a reasonably good relationship with most of the solicitors and barristers that I encountered. The vast majority were simply trying to do their best for their clients but did not lose touch with reality. On one occasion Mike and I had been conducting a distasteful inquiry into the activities of a paedophile who was responsible for sordid sexual activities with a number of young boys. He was a choir master at a local church and the children in his care he had been seducing. We eventually arrested him and, on his initial court appearance, the prosecutor opposed bail. The defence solicitor made a brilliant and impassioned plea on behalf of his client. He was so eloquent that he swayed the magistrates who eventually agreed to his release. The condition, however, was that he must reside at an address other than his own.

As we left the court precincts we were conversing with his solicitor and Mike could not resist poking fun at him.

'Hey, if he's such a nice guy why don't you take him home to stay with you?'

'You've got to be joking! I've got teenage lads, that pervert's getting nowhere near my home!'

Could he possibly be speaking about the man he had so robustly defended?

Chapter Fifteen

By May of 1974 Mike and I had been working as partners for some two years in the Regional Crime Squad. That month we were both promoted – me to detective inspector and Mike to detective sergeant. Even better, we were not being separated. Detective Chief Superintendent Tom Whittlestone, head of the CID, gave me the news personally and asked me where I would like to be posted. I did not hesitate – I immediately asked for Wavertree and my wish was granted. To my delight, Mike landed the same station. We were both returning to Murder Mile where I would be the CID commanding officer. This happy state of affairs was not destined to last long.

One evening I arranged to meet up with Mike at the Heath Hotel in Allerton. Mike was called to the telephone and he returned to tell me that a man had been shot in the Weighbridge pub in Wavertree Road and we were required at the scene. Initial inquiries revealed that he had not been shot but had been battered over the head with a shotgun. His head injuries were so severe I could understand why the first officers to respond had made that assumption. While I was still trying to sort it out in the bar, Tommy Whittlestone came in. At one time Tom had been our chief inspector. He had had to rein us in at times when our exuberance could have led us into trouble and he'd put up with our attempts to hoodwink him on many occasions. I was briefing him when Mike came over to give me some information.

'Boss,' he said to me, 'we've got an address for the guy who did this. Do you want me to get a team together and nick him now?'

Now, although Mike and I were close friends, protocol meant that if we were on duty at an incident he would never refer to me by my first name.

Tommy looked shocked and glanced from me to Mike and back again.

'What are you doing here?' he demanded of him.

'I'm here over this job, sir,' replied a bemused Mike.

'Good God, are you two in the same division? I didn't put you together again, did I?'

I know we had given him some grey hairs over the years but I still thought it was a bit over the top when, only days later, Mike was posted to another station! Especially as he had made an arrest for the attack later that same night.

Blags, if not a daily problem, were still a thorn in my side. We had more than our share of them – like the one that took place just after opening time one morning at a jeweller's shop in Allerton Road. Despite this being a busy area, thronged with shoppers, two young men had walked in, blatantly pulled out handguns and made off with stock amounting to many thousands of pounds. That very morning we were expecting a new detective who had been posted to Lawrence Road. His last station had been St Helen's, part of Lancashire Police, but unfortunately he was late in arriving. There had been a bomb scare on the East Lancashire Road and the highway had been closed down. He turned up at the robbery somewhat flustered. I told him what had occurred and that he may as well take responsibility for the investigation. I allotted him Detective Constable Graham Ledger to work the inquiry with him. When I had left he turned to Graham.

'Where's the control room set up?'

Graham looked at him bemused. Lancashire had so few incidents of such seriousness that manpower would be poured in to investigate it at length. In Liverpool it was just another job!

An indication of the work that the average detective got through in Liverpool was shown when one young detective applied to transfer to a force in a southern county. During his interview he was asked what his average case load was. He gave them a figure and the board members nodded and one commented that would be the average for their force as well. Only a little later did it transpire that they thought he was talking of the crimes he would be investigating per year. In fact he had given them his monthly total!

I gave Mike a hand with a search warrant in a road in Speke one morning. He had received information that the son who lived at the house had broken into a boutique the previous night and had stolen several thousands of pounds' worth of dresses. Under normal circumstances one of us would have covered the rear of the property but, because of the layout, it was impossible. As we walked down the path we braced ourselves. His mum was one of the most vitriolic people I had ever met, with an extremely short fuse. We were not to be disappointed.

After knocking for several moments and hearing hurried activity inside, the door was suddenly flung open.

'What do you two bastards want? You can piss right off! There's nothing here!'

'Morning, Debbie, I see that your education at Roedean College was wasted.'

'What?'

'Never mind, love. Come on, we've got a warrant to turn the house over.'

Reluctantly she stood aside and followed us around, muttering and cursing as we searched the premises. Our suspect sat in the kitchen glowering at us sullenly. Finding nothing of interest, we opened the door and walked into the rear garden. Strewn all over the grass were dozens of dresses from the burgled shop, still bearing the price tags. Debby stood there open-mouthed and for a second I thought she was going to faint. She was so overcome she even forgot to insult us when we arrested her for receiving and her son for the burglary.

I left Mike to deal with the interviews and I spoke to him later that night. He mentioned that both had made admissions and been charged. I asked why she was so shocked when we had found the gear.

'When we were trying to get in, they threw the property over the wall into next-door's garden.'

'Then how the hell did it get back where we found it?'

'Simple. The feller who blew them up to me lives there. He just flung it back over again!'

Debbie got sent down for a month for handling stolen goods. Some time later, Mike and I met up for a drink in the Dove and Olive near Speke airport. As we were chatting he asked me if I had heard the latest news on Debbie.

'When she was inside she formed a relationship with another woman. Came out a lesbian, left her husband and set up house with her new girlfriend!'

'Debbie? You must be joking, she was man-mad.'

'Straight up, I've seen them myself. The other girl's from Birkenhead. They've got a flat by Lark Lane nick. I was in the Masonic pub the other night. The pair of them were all over each other, couldn't keep their hands to themselves.'

'Her husband must be incensed about that. Watch yourself, he can be a nasty bastard in drink. He'll probably blame you for getting her sent down. The way he'll see it is that, if she hadn't, she would never have met this girl.'

'Well, I did hear he was looking for me. Seems he wants to buy me a few pints for getting shot of her for him!'

Chapter Sixteen

The night that seven-year-old Margaret was found slain in Wavertree, I had been enjoying a social evening at Fairfield Police Club at the senior CID officers' dinner night, completely unaware of the tragedy that had unfolded. Late that evening I saw Tony Frost, my detective superintendent, making his way through the crowd to my table.

'Mike, we have to go. We've got a murder on your patch.' Briefly he filled me in with what he knew and we arranged to make our way immediately to the scene. Hastily explaining what had occurred, I arranged for Carol to be taken home. Within minutes I was on my way, paying little, if any, heed to the speed limits. On arrival I was directed by a uniformed constable down a back entry along which Margaret had made her last walk on this earth and entered the rubbish-strewn and vandalised house. By now some portable lighting had been set up and I climbed the stairs to view the body. Margaret lay on her back, her eyes open, wearing a floral dress and white knee-length socks. A raincoat was fastened around her neck and I noted that both her shoes were halfway off her feet and a half-eaten chocolate bar lay near to her. It was dank, miserable and dark in the boarded-up house – a dreadful and frightening place for a little girl to end her days.

Tony arrived and we made a cursory examination of the scene as a forensic team began to swarm over it. I have often been asked how I felt attending such a tragedy. I always found that hard to respond to. Despair, most certainly. To see such a little scrap of humanity dead and with a complete lack of dignity, in such a dreadful place, can only bring the most intense feelings of compassion and sorrow. But never anger. That can only lead to a clouding of your judgement. Determination, most certainly. I would be prepared to work myself into the ground to bring her killer to justice. Many officers say that they are able to be completely detached, but I confess that not once did I feel that way.

Eventually I left the scene to set up the Murder Control Room. As always, following a particularly senseless killing, some part of me had changed for ever. Lawrence Road was only a short drive away and I went to my office on the first floor and began to put my mind to actions that had to be prioritised. Some detectives were already there, others were arriving by the minute. There was no such unit as a designated permanent Murder Squad. The inquiry was dealt with by the detectives responsible for the area in which a body was found, supplemented by officers drafted in from other divisions. Giving instructions for equipment to be brought in and offices to be made ready, I knew that Tony would arrive shortly. He needed to be briefed before the first conference for the investigation team, which would eventually number more than a hundred detectives.

This was my first murder case on my own patch in the rank of detective inspector. The responsibility covered me like a heavy cloak. Although part of a team, the outcome would be in my hands and I was only too aware of that.

Sitting behind my desk in my small cramped office, I lit the first of the countless cigarettes I would smoke that night. Ian 'Jock' Stewart, one of my senior sergeants, came in with two cups of coffee and I gratefully accepted one. Ian had been the first supervising officer on the murder scene and he outlined to me what had already been achieved. Having done this, he then told me of an arrest he had already made.

'After I called you and the boss out, I was told Margaret was last seen at a neighbour's house in Garrick Street. One of the lads in the house, Ernie, sent her and his sister on an errand. I had a word with him and didn't like the look of him. Anyway, for what it's worth, I did a check. He was wanted, so I've nicked him and he's in the cells.'

'D'you fancy him for the murder?'

'Dunno, nothing to say it's him. Bit of a funny guy but seems cool enough.'

I trusted Jock and his instincts. We had worked together in the Regional Crime Squad and I knew he was not a character who got easily carried away.

He explained that Ernie had a bit of a record, although nothing spectacular, and was married. He had been living with his wife and five-year-old child on the Netherely Corporation estate to the south end of the city. Some weeks earlier he had assaulted his young wife but had skipped prior to the arrival of uniformed officers.

Circulated as a wanted person, he had obviously been holed up at his parents' home, the house where Margaret had last been seen alive.

Tony arrived and, after I had brought him up to date, wheels were set in motion to have the inquiry up and running. We then came to the subject of our friend Ernie.

'So far as we know, Mike, he would have been one of the last people to see her alive. What does Jock think?'

'He's open-minded. I haven't seen Ernie myself. I was going to have a word when you arrived.'

'You better had. Look, I'll keep things going here. You and Jock have a chat with him and let me know what you think.'

I turned to go and, as I did so Tony remarked almost as an aside: 'Poor little kid, you can never get used to seeing them like that, can you?'

I shook my head sombrely and made my way out.

Just after 1 o'clock that morning I looked at Ernie on the other side of my desk. A scruffy-looking individual with lank greasy hair, he gazed sullenly at me as he drew nervously on his cigarette. I identified myself to him as Jock sat swinging his legs on the side of another desk. I confirmed that he was aware that Margaret was dead and that this was part of the investigation. In the initial interview he stated he had been home since about 3.30 p.m. the previous day, not leaving until about 10 p.m. when he had visited a local pub with his father.

'Do you know Margaret?'

'Well, I don't know her, like. Never seen her in my life before today. She was playing ball with our Paula in the hall this afternoon.'

'What happened then?'

'She left, didn't she?'

'What time was that?'

'I sent Paula for the *Echo* and gave her two bob for going. The other girl was there so I gave her two pence.'

'I would like you to make a written statement regarding this.'

'No, I never put anything in writing.'

'We're trying to trace the movements of the dead girl. All we want is for you to help us.'

'I'm not making no statement.'

We went over his alleged movements that day once more and I asked who could verify them.

'The family.'

'All the family?'

'No, me mum's in hospital, but me dad and the kids can.'

'Well, they'll have to be seen.'

'Why?'

'Are you still not willing to make a written statement?'

'Do I have to?'

'No one wants you to do anything you don't want to.'

'Well I'm not.'

'Are you adamant about that?'

'What?'

'Have you made your mind up about not making a statement?'

'Yeah.'

Jock took him back to the cells and we conferred again with Tony.

'What do you think?'

'I'm not certain, boss, there's something about him I

can't put my finger on. Why the hell won't he put his activities into writing? The *Echo* costs 5p doesn't it?'

'Yeah, why?' Jock asked.

'Why would he tip them so much for going for the paper? The shop's only on the corner. I just find that odd.'

'OK, Mike, have another go. Let's see what he's made of. We've interviewed some of his family and they don't agree that he was in all the time. We're having statements taken now but something's not right. Keep me posted. I'll keep things running here.'

As Jock left to fetch Ernie once more, neither of us knew that several further interviews were going to continue through the night. This time we put it to him firmly that his family were not agreeing with him. He was adamant he had not left the house.

'I never touched that kid. I've got a daughter of my own what I love. My marriage is gone but I miss my kid.'

'You gave us your family as your alibi. We told you that it would be checked and it doesn't look as if it's standing up.'

For several minutes he did not reply or look at me. He was clasping and unclasping his hands and sighing deeply.

'If I tell you the truth about it, a gang of bobbies will come in here and beat me up.'

'How do you mean?'

'They're probably outside the door now.'

'If you believe that go and have a look.'

'I believe you.'

'Nobody is going to touch you.'

'They will when I go down.'

'How do you mean?'

'If I tell you the truth and go to prison the other prisoners will beat me up for it. I know what goes on there.'

For the first time a chink was opening in his armour. He continued to sigh, along with lengthy silences. He then mentioned that after Margaret had left his home he had glanced through the window and seen her talking to a man. Another spate of sighing lasted for several minutes.

'Why are you sighing like this?'

'I want to tell you.'

'Tell us what?'

'It wasn't deliberate but I'm not saying it was me. Just let me think again on my own for a few minutes.'

By now the hairs were standing up on the back of my head. From his whole demeanour I was sure that we had the right man. Jock felt exactly as I did and we reported to Tony how the interview was developing. In company with him was a uniformed senior officer, a man I had little respect for and who showed little time for officers under his command. He showed his street wisdom in what he said to me.

'Do you think it could be him?'

'Early days yet, but there's something definitely odd about him.'

'I can't agree. I had a look at him in the cells and he doesn't look like a murderer to me.'

This was met with stunned silence. Exactly what does a murderer look like? He had absolutely no experience to base such a comment on. The looks of amazement that he received showed that all present agreed that this man was a prat.

We again spoke with Ernie, going over his alleged movements. He suddenly began to sigh and then blurted out: 'It wasn't deliberate you know. It was an accident how she died.'

'What do you mean?'

'What I said, but I'm not saying it was me.'

'If you never left the house and you say it was an accident, how do you know it was an accident?'

'If I tell you the truth now, your bosses will only make you twist it.'

'What do you mean?'

'You won't want to twist it but they'll make you.'

'Why should anyone want to twist the truth?'

'It wasn't murder, it was an accident. I'm still saying it wasn't me.'

'Well, how do you know it was an accident?'

'I can't answer that. I want to tell you about it because I want it to be easy, not the hard way.'

'Easy or hard?'

'Not the murder charge. It was an accident.'

'Well, what happened then?'

'I never left the house.'

Again he sank into a mood of depression, remaining silent other than sighing deeply.

'Can I have another cup of coffee?'

We gave him one and left him alone to think over his position.

Chapter Seventeen

Again we sat down with Tony and brought him up to date. It was agreed that we should continue the interviews after we had all had a rest. The next interview was a formality to establish that Ernie insisted that there had been no contact between him and the deceased. I also informed him that we intended to seize all his clothing for forensic examination. He again began to sigh and asked us to give him a couple of minutes. Just after 6 a.m. we had the last brief interview with him.

'You wanted us to leave you for a few minutes. Have you had long enough?'

'Yes, I just can't bring myself to tell you. I know what will happen to my clothes.'

'What is it you want to tell us?'

'It was an accident but I'm not saying it was me.'

'I feel at this stage there's no point in asking you further questions.'

'I want to tell you. I want to get it off my chest but I can't.'

It was decided now that we all needed a break. The function at which I had been so rudely interrupted seemed days earlier. Having come straight to the inquiry, I was still dressed in dinner jacket and black tie. I glanced around my office as Jock opened the windows to let the cigarette smoke out. As the fresh air blew into my face, I looked at the crammed ashtrays and shuddered as to how many we had smoked.

Shortly after 7.30 a.m., with bleary eyes, I queued to pay the toll to travel through the tunnel to my home on the Wirral. As I passed over the coins I caught the expression on the collector's face as he saw how I was dressed. It was one of contempt and disdain. He obviously thought I was a Jack the Lad on my way home from clubbing it all night. If only! After a quick shower and change of clothes, I ate a breakfast hastily prepared by Carol. I then gunned my Capri back down the motorway and shortly after 9 a.m. I was back behind my desk. Detective Constable John Jeffries brought me a coffee as I read over statements that had been taken in my absence. By now the murder was headline news locally and the national press and TV were inundating us with enquiries. A conference was held mid-morning and the day passed smoothly. It had been decided that further interviews with Ernie were of no advantage and later I charged him with the assault on his wife and he remained in custody.

Margaret's body had been identified at the mortuary by her father, a most harrowing experience for him. Murder has more than one victim. The suffering of the loved ones stays with them for the rest of their lives. Families are affected for ever when such a thing occurs. Margaret's mother and father were absolutely devastated.

A post-mortem had now established that the cause of

death was asphyxia, the mackintosh had been tied tightly around the girl's neck and fastened by a single knot. The time of death was estimated as being several hours before she had been found. Post-mortems are a vital aspect of such an investigation. However, I have always felt that such an examination is the final indignity brought to the victim. I detested having to attend them but consoled myself that, even in death, the victim was unknowingly helping me bring their killer to justice.

On Ernie's appearance at Dale Street Magistrates' Court a successful application for him to remain in custody was granted. I then saw him with Jock in the cells underground in the complex. At first he was asked some perfunctory questions.

'Do you remember telling us that you never left the house any time around five o'clock?'

'Yes. I never left the house.'

'We have reason to believe that, in fact, you stated to your sister that you were going for lemonade, is that true?'

'No, it isn't.'

'So when she says that you went out, having stated your intention to purchase lemonade, then returned and said you weren't paying eighteen or nineteen pence for it, that is untrue?'

He did not reply but began to sigh, staring at the floor and wringing his hands. After several minutes he spoke.

'Look, I couldn't sleep over this. I know I need to think before I tell you. I'm going to Risley and I want you to come up there and see me about it.'

We had by no means put all our eggs in one basket. Although Ernie's attitude was strange, we had absolutely nothing to connect him with the murder at this stage. In nearly every murder inquiry various people come into the frame, only eventually to be cleared of any suspicion. We had a completely open mind as we carried on with the investigation. The files on a number of previously reported sex attacks were again opened, more officers were drafted in, and again Carol saw little of me. I was out at 7 a.m. and never home before midnight. Panic swept the area. Children were not allowed to play outside and rarely ventured out of their concerned parent's sight. house-to-house inquiries had begun and information was pouring in from the public.

Risley Centre housed prisoners remanded in custody in the North West judicial area. By the time we went to see Ernie on Sunday, another weekend had gone and we knew that his account of his movements was beginning to fall about his ears. Suspicion and proof are, however, two different animals. We had also traced a 36-year-old married woman, Ann, with whom he had been having an affair. She told us that Ernie had been violent towards her and that he seemed to have an unhealthy obsession with one of her daughters. He had taken a photograph from her, cut part of it out which pictured her daughter and repeatedly kissed it, saying how beautiful she was and asking if he could take the girl out. One thing, she said, was very interesting. She had telephoned him at about 4.30 p.m. on the day of the murder but had to curtail the call. She had said she would ring back and he had asked her when, as he was going out. We had sightings of him away from his home on the day of the murder but they were from young children whose statements could obviously be challenged in the days ahead and could not be relied on in a future trial.

After my initial questions, I knew that I was now talking to a man who had had time to get his head together and was displaying some arrogance. Ernie told Jock and I that he knew who had committed the crime but was covering up for him.

'Is it a member of your family you're covering for?'

'No, you're completely wrong there.'

'Who then?'

'I'm not going to say. I know I'll get fifteen years for it but I'm not going to say who it was. I'll just take the blame.'

'It's not normal for a person to take the blame for a murder like this.'

'Unless they done it. I'm not saying it was me. You'll have to prove it, I'm not taking the easy way.'

'What do you mean by that reply?'

'I'm not saying any more about the murder to you.'

He was then questioned about goods recovered in his possession which had come from two burglaries where the properties had been set on fire. He admitted the offences but denied setting fire to the houses.

'Do you still refuse to discuss the murder further?'

'No, I don't want to talk about it. I'll take the blame. I'm not saying it was me. If I get done for it and get fifteen years it won't be on your conscience.'

'On my conscience?'

'Well, you should only have a conscience if the wrong person gets blamed. You don't have to worry about this.'

'What do you mean?'

'You know what I mean, I don't want to talk about it any more.'

Everything, especially the interviews, pointed to Ernie. Forensics had now established that the fibres on his clothing linked him to the murder scene and to the deceased. A fibre from her left thigh was also positive. The hard work of the search scene team had been well rewarded. Tony, Jock and I had a lengthy conference and the outcome was that we believed there was sufficient evidence to charge him. On the afternoon of Thursday, 6th March, Jock and I again saw him at Risley, the day before he was due before the Liverpool Magistrates' Court. He came into the room smiling and apparently very confident. Tossing his cigarettes onto the table, he leant back in his chair and placed his feet on the desk as he greeted us. I decided not to beat about the bush.

'I have made further inquiries into this matter. As a result, prior to your appearance before the court tomorrow I will charge you with the murder of Margaret and this is a copy of that charge that will be placed against you.'

There was a stunned silence, as various emotions from fear to rage raced over his face. He then sat there as if I had hit him with a sledgehammer. Eventually he recovered somewhat and looked intently at me, as if we were the only two people in the room.

'Can I talk to you on your own, Mr Mulloy? I'm not

being funny, Mr Stewart – Mr Mulloy will understand.'

Jock left the room and Ernie sat back, folded his arms and looked at me in a resigned manner. Although outwardly calm, my emotions were racing. Was this it? Was the hunt for the killer coming to an end? Trying to appear unconcerned I lit a cigarette and waited for him to speak.

'You've known all along it was me. I can't sleep because of what I've done to that little girl. It was me and I want to get it off my chest and tell you.'

My heart was pounding but I composed myself quickly.

'I'm calling Detective Sergeant Stewart back into the room.'

'I just wanted to tell you first. I think you understand me more as you're nearer my age.'

I went to the door and beckoned to Jock who took one look at my face and knew that it was over. Ernie said to him as he entered, 'I've just told Mr Mulloy that it was me. I'm sorry I didn't tell you before. I did it because of my little girl.'

He agreed to make a written statement under caution about the murder, which I wrote down as he dictated it to me. His version of the events was that he had broken into the electric meter at his parents' house and had stolen the cash contents and container. He had secreted the cash at 58 Webb Street, and on the day of the murder, had gone to collect some of the money. Unbeknown to him he had been followed by Margaret. She had seen him with the container and fearful she would tell his parents, he had simply killed her to ensure her silence. According to him, her life had been snuffed out for the sum of £28.50. Having added that he had tied the coat around her neck, he drew me a sketch which showed the location of the murder scene. As a result of what he said, later that day the electric container was recovered hidden, as he had told us, under the floorboards of the murder house. Details like these could only have been known to the killer. The final pieces of jigsaw had been slotted in.

Having obtained the confession, we left the interview room. When dealing with him we had displayed no emotion whatsoever. When we reached the corridor Jock picked me up in a bear hug and dance me around, he was so delighted. For over a week we had lived, eaten and slept with the inquiry. We had hardly been home other than to collapse for a few hours of snatched sleep, but our efforts had now been justified.

I telephoned Tony and told him what had gone on, before Jock and I travelled back to Liverpool. We met up at the murder control, where the team members were in a state of euphoria. A wave of tiredness overwhelmed me. All I wanted now was to get home and switch off. Jock lived near me so we travelled to the Wirral together and decided to have a quick drink to help us relax. Strangely, sitting in the Basset Hound in Thingwall, we had little to say to each other. We sat back, content that we had completed the inquiry. I was drained, having worked well over a hundred hours in the last few days. Even when I had snatched some hours in bed, I had tossed and turned, unable to close my mind about the next steps to be taken, reliving the inquiry in my mind. The first thoughts that had crowded into my consciousness as I woke had been about the murder.

I don't suppose it really hit me until I was travelling to work the following morning and the news came on the car radio accouncing that a man would be appearing in court that day charged with Margaret's murder. I heard it with mixed emotions, one of achievement, tinged with sadness at the demise of a little girl. I reflected just how much effort we had put in over a concentrated period of a few days. When I arrived at the office the pressure had hit Jock overnight. He was off sick, having woken up and found that he had lost a layer of skin from the roof of his mouth. This case, however, was to take yet another twist. On a remand appearance, Ernie told his solicitor he wanted to see Jock and I. He had changed his tune and now alleged that his father was, in fact, the murderer. His new version was that his father had returned home, admitted killing Margaret and told him where he had left the girl. Ernie had then gone to Webb Street and seen the body. He had told his father to say nothing, if necessary he would admit the murder on his behalf.

Well, it was different to say the least. A lot more work had to be done to establish that his father had not committed the murder. Eventually it became patently obvious that this story was completely false and Ernie's father was exonerated. Part of this later inquiry caused us to once more interview his married girlfriend, which revealed just how cunning Ernie really was. A few days before he made the allegation against his father, she had visited him while he was on remand. He had ordered her to send an anonymous letter to the police, alleging that his father was responsible, and have someone ring up anonymously and furnish a description of a man seen with Margaret about the time of her murder. Not surprisingly, the description he wanted passed on was one that would resemble his father.

On the morning the trial was due to begin, the defence requested a week's remand, which was granted. This caused me some problems as I was due to start my annual leave on this new date and Carol was expecting the pair of us to be in a hotel in Devon. Fortunately, I managed to get the booking amended when I rang begging for help to save my marriage!

On Ernie's subsequent appearance at the Crown Court at St George's Hall he pleaded not guilty. The trial was held in the magnificent surroundings of No. 2 court before Mr Justice Hollins. They were truly imposing halls of justice. In comparison, today's Crown Courts resemble airport lounges.

At least now Ernie did not blame his father. Basically, his defence was that Margaret had died at his hands but not intentionally, so he was seeking a manslaughter verdict. The Crown Prosecutor, Monty Dovenor QC, told the jury: 'You will probably think when you have heard the evidence that this was one of the most tragic and senseless killings ever to take place in this country.'

I gave my testimony and the trial eventually unfolded. Ernie alleged that he had been in the house when Margaret came up the stairs. She had asked what he was doing and he had sworn at her and told her to go away. He had placed his hand over her mouth then on to her neck. He didn't think he had hurt her until he tried to pick her up and there was no movement. He had tied the sleeves of her raincoat around her neck, panicked and ran off.

Monty pulled no punches in his cross-examination of him. 'This little girl, and she paid for it with her life, stumbled on the place where you had put the money. I suggest that you swatted her like a fly and then strangled her.'

The final speeches were made and the jury retired to consider their verdict. Jock and I queued for a coffee and we were just about to drink it when an usher rushed up.

'Your jury's back, Inspector Mulloy.'

Jock looked at me astonished. 'They've only been out twenty minutes, there must be a mistake.'

It was no error. It had taken them only that short time to decide that Ernie had murdered little Margaret. He was impassive as he was sentenced to life imprisonment, and our eyes met as he descended the stairs, but there was not even a flicker of recognition. It was as if he had already entered his own world.

Our work in the case was written up by our bosses and, some time later, Jock and I were awarded a Chief Constable's commendation for the inquiry. In those days you also received a small monetary award and we were granted the royal sum of £3. However, as I pointed out to Jock, we had to put it into the correct perspective. Beneath our announcement, another officer was commended and awarded £5 'for his outstanding work as a member of the Band Section'.

'Well, boss,' Jock commented, 'he probably blew his own trumpet.'

I had one last meeting with Ernie. He had been taken to Walton Prison and, a few weeks after his conviction, I was contacted by the security officers there. I was told that he wanted to see me, but they had no idea why he had made this request. Some days later, Jock and I paid him a visit and, after some initial chit-chat, I asked him what he wanted to see me about. To my surprise, he wanted to admit many more offences of burglary. I had no notion why he wanted to do so but why look a gift horse in the mouth? He gave us an idea of the areas he had been active in and we arranged to see him a few days later with the relevant crime reports.

When we returned he completely blanked us.

'I'm admitting nothing else to you.'

'Why get us here in the first place? You must have had a reason.'

'I just wanted to see you two again. I want to be able to picture your faces in the years to come.'

I have no idea what was behind this. Was it a threat of future revenge? Jock and I were aware that he was a dangerous and unstable man, how else can you describe a person capable of committing such a horrendous crime and retaining all the appearances of normality immediately afterwards? The following day I received a telephone call from his father.

'I'm going to complain about you going to see our Ernie.'

'Complain about what?'

'Calling him a burglar, he's not like that. He's honest, our Ernie!'

Chapter Eighteen

We had quite a few robberies on our patch but, although guns had been pulled a few times, it was nothing like what was happening in Toxteth. They were getting hammered. Within a three-month period they had suffered over 150 offences of robbery and assault. A large number of attacks were being made on pubs, post offices and, in particular, betting shops.

The method was simple but effective. Three or more masked thugs would rush into the premises armed with handguns, axes and baseball bats. By intimidation and the threat of instant violence large amounts of money were snatched. Where necessary, security doors were simply smashed down. Although on many occasions the premises were thronged with customers, such was the terror the thieves inspired that no witnesses would admit to seeing anything useful. Too many people had seen that even token resistance provoked a severe beating. The force the robbers used was way over the top of what was required to gain their ends. A number of victims had been beaten so savagely that they had been hospitalised.

The dread that followed such attacks meant that many of the staff simply packed their jobs in. Over the years, I have known several people who have never been the same after having been innocently caught up in such situations. In extreme cases, it can ruin lives for ever.

One morning I was summoned to see Tommy Whittlestone. I was shown into his office at HQ and he got straight to the point.

'I'm very concerned about these jobs in Toxteth, Mike. It's got out of hand and something's got to be done. I have spoken to Mr Sheron and we have come up with the idea of forming a squad to concentrate on them. I want you to run it from Essex Street. Pick your own men, whoever you want you'll get. Happy enough to do it?'

'Yes, sir. When do you want me to start?'

'Today. There were three more robberies over the weekend. Mr Sheron is waiting to see you at Speke.'

Nat Sheron was a boss I thought the world of and, within the hour, I was in his office discussing staff.

'How many do you want, Mike?' asked.

'I've thought about that on the way here. I only want a squad of eight.'

'It's your choice but I would have thought you would have needed more. There's a lot to do.'

'Yeah, but I reckon a small dedicated team of guys who will go through fire for us is the best choice.'

'OK. I guess you want Mike Johnson with you, so – who else?'

I had decided upon the people I wanted and named them. I also asked for Jan Cook who was posted to the city centre. She had impressed me when we had worked together at Lark Lane. I knew I could not only trust these officers but that they would be ready to work themselves into the ground for me and cheerfully accept any demands I might make of them. We all had mutual respect for each other.

By the early afternoon my team had all been pulled from whatever they were doing and we held a briefing at Essex Street. Trawling through the files, we could see that a pattern of robberies had developed. On Monday and Tuesday mornings, post offices were the target. On Thursday, Friday and Saturday, betting shops would be hit around the time of the last race when most cash would be on the premises. If only our lives were so simple.

The number of possible targets was so great it was impossible for us to carry out observations in the expectation of catching them in the act. I arranged with the Task Force, a specialised pool of officers which gave support to divisions, to assist us in observations when the pattern suddenly changed. Robbers are not stupid and word on the streets got back to us that they knew of our existence. Although the offences were prevalent, at least they were concentrated in one district. Our concern was that if they spread their wings throughout the city, we would have one hell of a difficult job.

As I saw it, our first task was to overcome the wall of silence that was protecting our robbers. In some of these premises, over fifty persons had been present but no one would admit to seeing anything. Even some informants, no strangers to violence themselves, were so intimidated that they were not forthcoming.

We hit the streets and called in favours we were owed and some we were not. I was used to long hours but the next six weeks were ridiculous. Often I got home just after dawn and I was always out until the early hours of the morning; my rest days were forgotten.

Carol was understanding about my absences but she had a subtle way of making a point if she felt I had stepped over the line. One morning, on returning in the early hours to my Prenton home, I found a note pinned to the bottom of the stairs: 'Mrs Mulloy's bed and breakfast. Favourable rates to police officers.'

The next morning she told me she had been driven to it as our cat, Fluffy, spat at me because he considered me a stranger and the neighbours were beginning to think that she had been widowed!

The first stage in our operation was discovering who we were looking for, the next was trying to find them. This would be achieved either by patrolling or putting doors in. As the arrests started, we were met with violence, insults and abuse. Undeterred, the squad pressed on and we got on a roll. From the outset of the inquiry we had a valuable contact assisting us. She worked as a barmaid in one of the more notorious clubs and knew everyone in the area. An attractive and voluptuous girl, she was also very shrewd and missed nothing. Mike and I had dealt with her for a couple of years and now she proved invaluable.

One of the first men we got our hands on from her information was typical of those we were hunting. He was wanted for his part in attacks on a post office and a betting shop in Toxteth during which firearms had been produced and the staff threatened. Some weeks earlier he had been arrested in connection with these robberies and, although placed into a police car, he had violently attacked the two divisional detectives. He went absolutely berserk and the struggle was so violent that he had his clothes completely torn off him. Absolutely naked, he had smashed through the rear window of the car and literally 'streaked away'. One officer was left unconscious, the other suffered deep lacerations. Our informant told us where this man was hiding out and, just after dawn, we hit a flat in Englefield Green. Screaming threats and clad only in his shorts, our target raced down the stairs and attacked us with a heavy piece of metal. After a violent struggle, he was overpowered and taken into custody.

We began to get confidence back on the streets and information started to come in, followed inevitably by arrests. A lot of our street knowledge came from the local prostitutes who wanted the whole affair finished because we were bad for business, out at all hours and watching what was going on.

Mike and I were having a final cruise along Upper Parliament Street just after 3 a.m., both aware we were due at the Crown Court only six hours later. Just as we passed Grove Street we came across a car parked in the middle of the carriageway with the lights on and the driver's door ajar. Presuming we had come across an abandoned stolen vehicle, we alighted to carry out a check. Mike radioed the number to the control room and we waited to see what was known.

'Hello, is that the police?'

'Who the hell is that?' Mike asked. We looked around but, apart from us, the street was deserted.

'I'm down here.'

We realised that the disembodied voice was coming from the cellar area of one of the old houses.

Crouching there, we found a very frightened middle-aged man and his story was a familiar one. He had been naive enough to pick up two local prostitutes and had been on his way to a secluded spot to enjoy their favours. His hopes had been dashed when they produced knives and robbed him of his wallet and watch. He had leapt from the car and, in fear, had taken refuge where we had found him.

We put him in the back of the squad car and made a tour of the area. He positively identified his two attackers among a crowd of people coming out of clubs by the Rialto. Both women were well known to us, they had been at it for years, and we nicked them. We found his property on them so they both joined us for the trip to Essex Street.

One was Sonia – a most charming female. I would guess that she was probably the most objectionable, foul-mouthed woman I have ever met. She was only too happy when she was creating a scene. Mike had charged both of them and as the offence was one of robbery, the case could not be dealt with by the Magistrates' Court. Because of its seriousness, the matter could only be dealt with at the Crown Court. Many weeks later, she was due to appear to have her case heard but that morning Mike was up to his eyes with work. One of the young detectives in his office was also going to the court over another case and he readily agreed to look in and get the result for Mike's file.

Sonia appeared before a court crowded with barristers, solicitors, police officers and the public. Amazingly, she was very polite and pleaded guilty. Even when sentenced to eighteen months she thanked the judge for being fair to her and, instead of her usual ranting, she turned quietly to go down the steps to the cells. On the top step she paused and looked directly at the young detective, who had had no previous dealings with her.

'As for you,' she shouted, 'that's the last free wank you'll get off me!'

So saying, with a triumphant smile she swished down the stairs, leaving a very embarrassed young man to face the sniggers.

As the arrests began to mount up, the boot was now on the other foot. Fearing their turn was about to come, suspects vanished from their usual haunts and we engaged in protracted inquiries to hunt them down. Squad officers travelled to Cumbria, Lancashire and the Home Counties to effect their arrests. Our activities were so successful and intensive that once we had got up and running, such robberies simply ceased to be committed.

Late one evening we hit a house in Conleach Road in Speke, looking for a suspect called Johnny. We knew he was one of those responsible for an audacious robbery at a Toxteth public house. During the late evening, when the premises were packed, five masked men had entered, one was armed with a handgun with which he threatened the customers. The men demanded the takings, and when the licencee was slow to comply with their orders, they attacked him with broken bottles and iron bars. He had suffered a broken arm and cuts to his scalp and face which required numerous sutures.

The initial search of the house revealed nothing but Mike and one of the lads climbed into the loft. They shone their torches into the cold water tank and there, clad only in his underpants, was our quarry.

'Good evening, Mr Johnson. Can I help you?'

Johnny was hauled out and accepted his fate. This did not apply to his neighbours. A large crowd had gathered and, not for the first time, we had to fight our way out. A hail of bricks and bottles greeted us as we left with him in handcuffs. One of our vehicles was badly damaged but, apart from some cuts and bruises, we came through unscathed.

One of our informants was able to tell us that Gerry was hiding out somewhere in Widnes in the Cheshire County police area. We wanted Gerry for a number of jobs where he had been one of the gunmen. Although out contact was unable to get an address for us, she told us that Gerry drank most lunchtimes in the Red Admiral in nearby Runcorn. One problem was that he had no record so, apart from a description, we had nothing to go on. Wild horses would not have dragged the girl there to help identify him but she gave us one further piece of information – part of the registration number and the model of his car of which, apparently, he was inordinately fond.

A couple of days later the squad visited the pub and there in the car park, gleaming in all its glory, was our suspect's vehicle. Mike and I wandered inside for a drink. The place was crowded, our man could have been any one of a number of customers and it's a big pub. We joined up with our team and I took Jan to one side. After I had finished speaking to her, she nodded and left us with a big grin.

'What's going on?' Mike asked.

'Wait and see, Mike. I think he'll be out soon.'

We watched as Jan parked one of the squad cars with the front wing alongside the door of the suspect's vehicle. She then vanished into the pub. Within seconds a male burst out of the doors and ran to examine the vehicles. Stepping from our cars, we took him into custody. He was stunned, so much so that there was only token resistance – he knew that he'd been 'had over'.

After staging what looked like a minor collision, Jan had entered the pub and asked the barman to shout for the owner of the car she had allegedly clipped. Pride in his car had overtaken Gerry's natural caution!

Not all of my schemes with Jan have had such a happy result. Many of our more valuable contacts were prostitutes who lived an itinerant life style. The only place we could be sure to find them was on their patch and, naturally, they did not wish to be seen in the open talking to us. At my request, Jan agreed to hit the streets posing as one of the girls. To this end she made herself up heavily, donned a blonde wig and the appropriate, if somewhat skimpy, clothing. This was not an easy task that I was asking of her. The street is a dangerous place and if she had been rumbled she could have expected instant violence. Although Jan was always in sight of at least one squad member, she was still taking one hell of a chance.

We need not have worried. Jan was not only attractive, her vivacity and freshness shone out, so much so that she could only walk a few yards before a kerb-crawler was after her. They must have thought that all their dreams had come true. She attracted so many punters that we called it off.

As Mike dryly commented to me, 'The Vice Squad shouldn't nick anyone who approaches our Jan.'

'Why not?'

'They should nick those who drive past her. If they don't fancy her they must be paedophiles!'

Six weeks after the dust had settled on the Toxteth robberies, we were able to sit back and see what the squad had achieved. First and foremost, with over sixty arrests including fifteen top-level robbers, the type of offence we were investigating had ceased completely in the area. The arrests were for a wide range of offences, not only robbery but also for grievous bodily harm and burglary. A variety of weapons including firearms, knives and machetes had been taken off the streets. Several hundred serious crimes had been detected, not only on our patch but also in Cumbria, Cheshire, Lancashire, London, Brighton, Margate, Carlisle and Scotland. And in excess of £100,000 worth of stolen goods had been seized for eventual return to the rightful owners. One surprising statistic was that on no occasion when we conducted searches or made arrests had we been armed.

Many years of imprisonment were subsequently handed down for these nasty, cowardly offences. There was no doubt that the squad had caused massive ripples in the criminal pool. Rightly, every officer received a commendation from the Chief Constable. The citation read: 'For excellent work leading to an outstanding record of arrests for robberies and serious crime in such a short period of time.'

There is no doubt that such a superb conclusion to an inquiry had rarely been achieved so quickly. My squad had done the work of three times their number and now looked forward to a well-earned break. Now the task that we had been given had been completed I took the lads and Jan out for a drink. We had lived, eaten and slept the job and I had lost count of the hours and days we had put in for nothing. Mike drained his glass and started to laugh.

'What's so funny?'

'Have you read what's in the Chief Constable's orders today?'

'No, what?'

'From the end of the month, all future overtime will be paid for in full.'

'Why smile? We've just lost a fortune.'

'Not really. If they'd had to pay us, do you think those clowns at HQ would have let us do those mad hours?' Ruefully, we all had to agree.

The Monday after the squad was closed down I had to drop the report on their activities off to HQ. Mike was also due to visit so I picked him up at Essex Street so we could travel together. I was manoeuvring into the traffic flow in Park Road when I was called on the radio to attend a death on the railway lines at Wavertree. Mike agreed to come with me and we drove to the Edge Hill district. Climbing down the embankment, we were met by a grim-faced uniform sergeant with two ashen-faced young constables.

'It's a bad one, boss,' he told us. He went on to explain that the body was that of a fifty-year-old man who had a history of mental depression. He had lived locally and earlier had been seen walking along the side of the tracks. Several workmen had seen him deliberately step in front of a train, giving the driver no chance to avoid him. In such an incident a senior CID officer was required to attend, along with a police doctor who would certify death. Only then could the remains be removed.

Mike and I walked along the track and after turning a slight bend, we came across the body or, rather, what remained of it. There must have been a hell of a collision. The body was decapitated and some of the limbs had been torn off in the violent impact. Mike and I hurriedly lit cigarettes and I was definitely regretting the cooked breakfast I had enjoyed so recently in the Allerton canteen. We spoke to the witnesses and established that this tragedy carried no suspicious circumstances.

Eventually the doctor arrived and stood over what was left of the body. Other than wishing us good morning he was silent for several moments before spoke. At last he gave us his considered medical opinion.

'Do you really need me to tell you he's dead?'

'No, you sarcastic sod, I don't. But I bet it won't stop you claiming the expenses for coming here!'

He stormed away from us and surveyed the dreadful scene for several moments in silence. Both of us knew that we had one more chore to complete.

'OK, Mike, better get the blankets. I'll get the head.'

I swallowed back the rising bile as we went about our task. I never forgot that we were dealing with a human being, who in death still deserved to be treated with dignity. Having collected the remains, we drove away in silence. There are some things that are better not spoken about. It was not the first or last time we had to deal with such horror. Each of us in our own way dealt with our feelings and came to terms with how to handle it.

Chapter Nineteen

I was passing through the front office of the station one evening and accepted the offer of a cup of tea from the station sergeant. As we chatted, the front doors swung open and the senior duty officer from another station entered. He nodded curtly to me and I responded with the briefest of nods myself. When I had been a sergeant in the Regional Crime Squad I had worked out of HQ, where he had then been based. On several occasions when I had first started there I had passed him in the corridors of power. He never responded to my greetings. I would not have minded had he pretended he had not seen me but he would pause, then let his glance pass right through me as if I did not exist. After this had happened a couple of times I just ignored him. When news came through that I had been promoted to the rank of inspector things changed. By chance, the very next morning I came across him in the canteen.

'Good morning, Mike, congratulations. How are you?'

I looked at him for a few seconds before I responded to his greetings.

'I'm sorry if I seem perplexed but for nearly two years you have ignored my existence and now you're hoping I'm well.'

'That was different. Now you're one of us – a senior officer.'

'If by being "one of us" means being ignorant, no thanks. I wasn't good enough for you yesterday and I haven't changed.'

Glaring at me the superintendant strode away and Mike said that I had made an enemy there. I wasn't too perturbed as I considered him a buffoon. What occurred next did little to change my opinion.

In those days cars had to display parking lights. The failure to do so was, naturally, a crime, high up on a policeman's list of priorities. In an inner-city policing area, they had little else to spend their time upon!

'Sergeant, there are a number of cars parked at the side of the station without displaying the requisite lights. Send your desk constable out to book them.'

To no avail the sergeant tried to explain to the superintendant that these were police officers' cars. The late shift had come on duty that afternoon, in the daylight, and obviously parked without lights on when they went out on patrol. He suggested that he call the officers back to put the lights on but he was wasting his time with this man.

Reluctantly the desk constable, an officer of nearly thirty years service, left the station to record the offending cars with a view to summonsing the owners. On his return, the superintendent examined the details he had recorded.

'Now, Constable, I will be checking that these have been forwarded with a decision to be made as to prosecution, don't think I won't.'

A full file was forwarded over this ridiculous incident

and the Chief Constable showed what he thought of it when all the officers received a formal letter of caution for parking without lights. At least he showed a sense of proportion.

Jock Stewart and I happened to be on night duty at the same time. As the senior duty officer, I was responsible for the entire area that the force covered. I had made arrangements to meet up with him and at dawn we were parked up at the Pier Head. As we sipped our coffees from the all-night refreshment stall we looked over the river, watching the sun rise to herald a beautiful morning. As we chatted, I was telling Jock that as a very young man I had worked on those docks and had probably learnt more about real life than at any other stage in my life.

I was already thinking of my bed when my reverie was disturbed by an urgent radio call to attend the Royal Infirmary. A 21-year-old constable had been a passenger in a police car when he and his partner had seen two men acting suspiciously in the Breck Road area of Everton, near to Goodison Park football ground. They had gone to check them out and both men had fled. The young officer had caught one of the fugitives and began to question him. Without any warning, or a chance to defend himself, a knife was suddenly plunged into his stomach. The attacker ran off and his victim was found in a pool of blood by his fellow officer and rushed to hospital. I was unable to interview him as he was to undergo an immediate operation and the medical staff would not commit themselves on the seriousness of his injury. I felt the same as any street officer, an attack on one of us always brought home the dangers of the job most vividly. He was a young married man with a family and now lay injured in a hospital bed.

Jock and I went to the scene of the attack in Brunai Walk and found a number of uniformed officers already present, along with their sergeant. I instructed an immediate search of the area and we had an early result when a bloodstained knife with a six-inch blade was found.

'Have you started house-to-house inquiries yet? Someone may have seen or heard something to help us.'

'Well, no. We can't really can we?'

'Why not?'

'They'll all be asleep.'

'Are you asleep?'

'No, sir.'

'OK, if you're awake get them up. May I remind you, one of your lads got bloody stabbed here. Get them on the knockers!'

I pointed to a small block of flats and told him that Jock and I would start there. We went through the communal door ready to give people an early morning wake-up. As the doors swung closed behind us, Jock and I stiffened. From the end of the deserted corridor we had both distinctly heard a slight scuffling noise. Putting my fingers to my lips in a warning gesture, Jock and I crept towards the stairs. Under the stairwell we saw the form of a man crouching down in an attempt to conceal himself, his jacket pulled over his head. We dragged him out and the first thing I saw was blood on his hands and his jacket. Before we could speak to him, he began to shout.

'I didn't stab the copper, honest!'

Jock nicked him and we took him to Eaton Road station where he was placed in the cells. The procedure on night duty over such an incident was clearly laid down. As inquiries into such a serious matter could take many hours, the onus for follow-up inquiries lay with the officers responsible for the area. By 7 a.m. we had done as much as we could – the scene had been searched and examined by forensic officers and photographs taken and, most importantly, there was a suspect in custody. We had conducted an initial interview with the man and by now he had told us who his mate was. The time had come to pass it over to the division so I got on the telephone. Twenty minutes later I replaced the receiver, all relevant officers had been informed and were on their way. It was time to get some sleep.

A couple of nights later I was called to Walton Hospital after the report of an attempted strangulation. A constable was guarding a side ward of the emergency admissions and there, in a bed, I found an attractive young woman. A deep weal ran completely around her neck and she had trouble speaking to me because of the damage to her larynx The duty doctor was treating her and he was shortly joined by the police surgeon, Maurice Kirwan. I waited until they had completed their examinations and, when they had done so, they were unanimous in their opinion. Both doctors were astonished that she had actually survived the attack. The depth of the wounds on her neck could well have been expected to extinguish her life.

The matter had begun as a domestic incident with the woman's ex-husband who was now in custody and I interviewed him briefly. In some respects this was an everyday tale of life in a big city. Two lives could have so easily have been ruined for ever that night. It was also typical of the sort of work required of men when on night duty. It was important to get the priorities sorted before calling out the officers from the division to complete the investigation after they had enjoyed some sleep.

Detective Sergeant Frank Carthy was the first divisional man to arrive in response to the inevitable phone calls regarding this matter. A great character, with a very dry sense of humour, nothing could faze him. Frank had originally been a member of Bootle when it was a borough force, infamous for its penny-pinching habits. Liverpool City detectives had once been attached there to assist in a murder and had been expected not only to provide their own stationery, but also to return to Liverpool stations if they felt the need to make telephone inquiries!

This parsimonious attitude also carried on down to the lower ranks. Frank once told me that, as a young constable on night duty, he had disturbed two well-known thieves in the act of breaking into a warehouse on the Dock Road. Both had fled, with Frank hot on their heels, and he soon caught up with one. After a violent struggle he had overcome him, handcuffed him to some railings, and carried on the chase for his colleague. This was well before the advent of personal radios, so Frank was entirely on his own.

After a pursuit of more than a mile Frank caught the second guy and was again violently assaulted before effecting his arrest. It was a good arrest of two criminals who had not hesitated to attack a police officer. When he arrived at the station with his two captures both his sergeant and inspector were fulsome in their praise. At the end of his shift, a tired and bruised constable went home and retired to some well-earned rest.

Just after 11 a.m. he was roused from his slumbers by his wife who told him that a sergeant was at the house needing to speak to him urgently. Befuddled, Frank went downstairs and was told him that a senior officer wanted him to attend at his office at noon, to speak with him over his arrest of a few hours ago.

Frank hastily washed and shaved and dressed in his best uniform. He pedalled to the station, his thoughts full of commendation and glory. After all, it was not every day that a boss wanted to see a young man so urgently. On his arrival he was ushered into the great man's presence. After Frank had been kept waiting, standing to attention before the senior officer's desk while he perused the night report, the man eventually looked up.

'Now Carthy, about this arrest of yours last night . . .'

'Yes sir,' responded a very proud Frank.

'How dare you risk the loss of police property? Have you any idea how much handcuffs cost? Leaving a man handcuffed – they could have been stolen!'

Frank suffered a tirade of similar comments before being summarily dismissed. Man management was obviously not a priority in that borough.

Chapter Twenty

Although I am not really superstitious, some dates remain fixed in my mind. Friday, 13th June 1975, which was four days before my birthday, is such an example. I had spent the day at the Crown Court and I was eventually released just after 3 p.m. I decided to spend a few hours in Carol's company before returning to work. I wasn't on duty that night but I had arranged a meeting with an informant who was assisting me regarding some armed robberies. I'd missed lunch, so Carol prepared me a snack of soup and toast. I had just lifted the spoon to my lips when the phone rang. I was greeted with the usual apologetic 'Sorry to bother you, boss,' and I listened intently to one of my detectives, Dave Montieth. Within minutes I was speeding down the M53 towards the Liverpool tunnel.

Strathcona Road is off Picton Road, less than a mile from the police station. A street of neat terraced homes, most of the residents had lived there for many years. One was occupied by Gertrude, an 83-year-old woman who was cohabiting with 63-year-old James. She had lived there all of her adult life and the couple were respected and popular in the area. They were well-liked regulars at the local pub, the Sandown Arms, and were always ready to help neighbours in any way they could. Despite her years, she was a spritely lady, full of life and always ready for a laugh.

Just after 2.30 p.m. that day, a girl and her fiancé were leaving their home in the street when they saw a young man peering through the glass panel of Gertrude's front door. They noticed that in his left ear lobe he was wearing an earring in the shape of a cross. At about this time the same young man was seen ringing the doorbell of the house. Gertrude opened the door and admitted him into her home.

Moments later, neighbours heard shouting and frantic screams coming from the house. Some of them rushed out and began to hammer on the front door, desperately ringing the bell. So blood-curdling were the sounds from within that one neighbour rushed to his car and armed himself with a hammer. He dashed to the rear entry and saw that the yard door to the house was ajar. Immediately prior to this a elderly lady had seen a man with his jacket pulled over his head running along this entry and out of her sight.

A neighbour clambered onto the front window-sill and saw Gertrude lying on the floor of the lounge. Another neighbour began to scream for the police and ambulance as more residents responded to the alarm. Amazingly, as they tried to force entry, Gertrude managed to gain her feet and and stumbled to the front door, which she opened before she collapsed into the arms of her friends.

The horrified helpers saw that she had sustained sickening injuries, including a gaping hole in her forehead. She was absolutely covered in her own blood.

Desperate attempts were made to render first aid, but she soon lapsed into unconsciousness. On the arrival of the emergency services, Gertrude was rushed to Sefton General Hospital and immediately placed into intensive care. She was having breathing difficulties because of the blood she had inhaled and was placed on to a ventilator. Ominously, examination revealed generalised brain damage. She was also suffering from fractures to several ribs. She had suffered what was described as a 'floating fracture' of her face. So severe was the attack the facial and nasal bones had been shattered, so the entire front of her face was no longer supported by her skull.

Being aware that at the hospital a medical team would be swarming over the injured old woman, I first made for the house where she had been attacked. I found a scene of carnage. Blood was spattered over the entire ground floor, on the walls, furniture and fitments and even the ceilings. The bloody hand-prints on the walls were silent signs of the desperate fight for life that had gone on. The large pools of blood already seeping into the carpet bore witness that the main attack had occurred in the living room, after Gertrude had been chased from room to room.

Having ensured that forensic examination was under way to my satisfaction, I drove to the hospital. After a delay I was able to see the victim. She was unconscious and barely recognisable, her face having swollen to twice its normal size. I was updated as to her condition, but even at that stage there was little confidence she would survive because of the severity of the attack and her age. Not for the first, or last, time I grimly tried to comprehend how one human being could inflict such horrific injuries on another.

From the outset the investigation was treated as if it was already a murder inquiry. Detective Superintendent Gordon McKenzie, deputy head of the CID, attended, and the control room was set up at Lawrence Road. Detectives were called in from throughout the force to form the squad.

Most of us had missed our meal, so later that night a young detective was sent to the local Chinese take-away for an extensive order. On his return he was laden down with a number of food cartons. 'Don't rush,' he shouted, 'take your time. I had the woman write on each container what's inside, so just take what you ordered.' Well that was true, only it didn't really help much. She had recorded what each package contained . . . in Chinese!

Although such an attack always strikes at the heart of a community, seldom have I known it have the effect it had on this tight-knit one. A torrent of information was rushing in and a lot came from the Sandown Arms. As part of the inquiry I visited the pub, speaking to the licencee, staff and many of the customers. If anything, the local population wanted the attacker just as badly as we did.

As the manhunt continued, Gordon was a regular visitor to the control room. He was a boss I respected greatly. However, any idea he came up with he wanted implementing and God help you if it wasn't. An example occurred on this investigation. He wanted a police presence in the intensive care unit, the thought being that if Gertrude recovered consciousness briefly she might give us a lead to her assailant. I was given the task of arranging it and my first stumbling block was the consultant in charge. He was obviously a very intelligent person but no gentleman. Frankly, and I quote, he was not having any 'hairy-arsed bobby' in his unit. He eventually succumbed to my entreaties and agreed to have an officer stationed outside who could be summoned by the staff should Gertrude wake up.

After his initial grumbling had subsided, even Gordon reluctantly conceded that I had achieved as much as I could.

'You know what the trouble with these medical people is, don't you, Mike?'

'No, boss, not really.'

'All they're interested in is getting people better, they don't give a hoot who did it.'

To some extent I could see his point but if I had been in their hands I know what I would have wanted to be their priority!

From the outset we had obviously been interested in speaking to the man who had been seen to call at the house. We were heartened by the sighting of the earring – at that time male jewellery was nowhere near as popular as it is today. The massive press coverage had stressed this point and, boy, did it get results. To our amazement we were inundated with calls. People were ringing up from pubs all over Liverpool, reporting customers in the bar with an earring! It came to the point that if you wore one it wasn't safe to leave the house. Some poor guys were informed about on several occasions and had to run the rigmarole of questioning yet again!

Murders are seldom solved by a shrewd piece of

deduction. Mostly a result is obtained at the end of a long hard slog of routine inquiries. This investigation was to be no exception. After several days of long hours without break, it was accepted that the final hour of a shift would be done in a pub so that the officers could at least unwind. Detective Constables Colin Case and Ken Isherwood were approaching the end of a long, fruitless day with just one person left to visit.

Alan was a 21-year-old who lived in the Huyton area of Liverpool. He had a very tenuous connection with the inquiry, his family having known James, Gertrude's partner, when they had lived in the area some years earlier. It was a bread-and-butter matter and although all the other family members had been seen, Alan had not yet been questioned. The lads decided to give it one last go and just after ten in the evening, they called at his home. As he came to the door all tiredness left them – to be replaced by a surge of adrenaline. In his left ear lobe he wore a silver crucifix. Within a very short time he was accompanying them to Lawrence Road.

It already looked very promising. Alan had told the officers he had called at the address on the day of the attack but that when he left Gertrude was in perfect health. All could now well rest on the forthcoming interview.

Chapter Twenty-One

Roy Horton and I led Alan to the interview room at the end of the corridor on the first floor. Not a bad-looking lad, tall and slim with blond hair, he seemed at ease with himself and his surroundings. We opened the interview and he agreed that he had called at Gertrude's house on the day in question to see James.

'I only went to see Jimmy but he wasn't in so I left after a few minutes.'

'Do you know Gertrude?'

'I don't really know her well but I do know she lives with Jimmy.'

'Why did you call at the house?'

'I've told you, to see Jimmy.'

'What did you want to see Jimmy about?'

'Just to say hello.'

'Have you called to see him at this house before?

'No, not for ages anyway.'

'What happened when you called?'

'The old woman told me that Jimmy wasn't at home and she asked me in. That's all that happened.'

'Did you talk to her?'

'Not really. I only stayed a little while, then I left.'

'Which way did you leave the house?'

'I was in a hurry so I left by the back door.'

Alan went on to give us an account of meeting his brother and Roy and I looked at each other. It was him. He was the man seen in the entry with his coat over his head, there was little doubt about that. I returned to the offensive.

'How does it save you time to leave by the back way?'

There was a prolonged silence.

'Did something occur at the house that made you want to leave quickly?'

'It wasn't me, if that's what you mean.'

'When did you know that the woman had been attacked in the house you called at?'

There was utter silence and I repeated the question.

'How bad is she?'

'She's in a critical condition.'

He then gave a further detailed account of his movements after he had left the house. He told us that he had gone shopping with his brother in the city centre. He was obviously more at ease talking about anything but the house visit. I put him on the back foot again.

'Back to when you called at Strathcona Road. Why were you in the area?'

He explained that he had been drinking with a friend in the Salisbury and Waldorf pub before calling on Gertrude. By now it was obvious that he did not want the interview to touch on his visit to the house. His demeanour when speaking about that was totally different from talking about other activities. I was determined to press on and eventually we reached a climax.

'You've told us that you didn't really talk to the

woman in the house. What did you say to her and what did she say to you?'

'I don't want to remember. I want to forget that day.'

'I've already told you that you don't have to say anything at all but I feel that you're not telling the truth about your visit to that house.'

'It's my headaches.'

'What headaches do you mean?'

'I get headaches but I don't want to say what happened.'

'Did you have a headache that day?'

'Yes, I get dizzy spells.'

'When did you last have a headache?'

'That day, the day the old lady was hurt.'

It was time to get down to the crux of the matter. Taking a deep breath I carried on. 'Tell me what happened at the house.'

'I had a headache before I called.'

'OK, what happened then?'

'I did it to the old lady because of my dizzy spells.'

'What did you do?'

'I was in the house and then I remember kicking her and she was lying on the floor. I ran out the back way and I remember crying in an entry near there somewhere. Then I went to meet our kid.'

'You went straight to meet your brother from the house in Strathcona Road?' I asked incredulously.

'I couldn't do anything about it, could I? I'd done it, so I decided to put it out of my mind.'

Alan added that he had washed the bloodstains from his clothing later that day and told us where in his home they could be located. He then went on to make a full written statement in which he confirmed everything that he had told us. It was over. We had our man.

Roy spoke as we left the interview room. 'Boss, how the hell can you do something like that then just carry on as normal?' I shook my head as I had no answer for him. I could still see her battered face in my mind.

We walked back into a crowded control room. Word had spread and just about every one on the inquiry had hastened back for news. Gordon looked at me quizzically and I gave him a slight smile and nodded. He pumped my hand and a wave of euphoria swept the room. Every officer, quite rightly, felt that he or she had brought about the result. Murder inquiries are a team effort with no individual stars.

DC Jim McCafftey called me over to the window in the general office.

'When the news gets out, the pubs are going to be busy tonight boss,' he said, gesturing out of the window.

I looked out into Lawrence Road and I was amazed by the crowd that had gathered on the pavements and was flowing into the road. Word had obviously got out that a man was in custody.

I chased the squad out. They had grafted long and hard and well deserved an early break. I remained with Roy, Jim, Ray Murray and Graham Ledger and we began completing the paperwork that had to be prepared. The silence was interrupted by the phone.

'DI Mulloy, can I help you?'

It was the licencee of the Sandown on the other end. He had heard the news and several of my lads were already relaxing there. Judging by the background noise, so was half of Wavertree. He only rang off when

I promised I would look in on the way home. He was most sympathetic that we would not be having a drink as we were tied up in the office. Some fifteen minutes later, a uniformed officer brought up a box which had been handed in at the front desk. Inside were several bottles of spirits with a card. It said simply: 'To the boys and girls of the CID at Lawrence Road. Thank you. The Sandown Regulars.'

I had never come across such a spontaneous gesture before and I confess it brought a lump to my throat. These people were not wealthy but I was later to learn that there had been a stampede to contribute for us.

Normally, I would have gone straight home. I always felt mentally and physically drained at the end of such an inquiry, as if a switch had been turned off. A bath, a decent meal and a quiet drink with Carol was what I most desired. However, with what had occurred it would have been churlish, so I made a detour and visited the pub. I only stayed for one drink as the reception we got was embarrassing, it was so fulsome. Promising to call back as soon as possible, I headed for my personal sanctuary.

The following morning at the Main Bridewell, I charged Alan with attempted murder. He was remanded in custody, but our inquiries continued before the file was closed. His fingerprints were by now positively identified at several locations in the house. Some were among the bloody hand-prints at the scene. Although attempts had been made to wash away traces, his clothing was spattered with blood from the victim.

What was unusual was that although he had been seen by family and friends immediately after the attack, throughout the afternoon and evening he showed no change in his usual demeanour. From the time of the assault onwards, it appeared he had been able to block the nightmare completely from his mind. I had to prepare a full file for the Director of Public Prosecutions and, to keep the peace, I had brought the report home with me. I had just added the final paragraph when Roy rang me, just after 11 a.m. on Sunday, 6th July 1975. Gertrude had succumbed to her injuries and passed away in the early hours without regaining consciousness. We now had a murder case. In truth, it was what I had expected. The following day a post-mortem was carried out and the thought crossed my mind that she had died without knowing we had her assailant in custody. Her partner, Jim, was devastated when we broke the news to him. He aged before our eyes.

'She can't be dead, Mr Mulloy, I've just decorated the parlour for when she comes home.'

The broken man spoke in shock. Gretrude was not the only victim.

Alan later appeared at the Crown Court before Mr Justice Kilner-Brown. He pleaded not guilty to murder, but guilty to manslaughter on the grounds of diminished responsibility. His plea was accepted and he was sentenced to life imprisonment. Another sad chapter of my service had closed.

Chapter Twenty-Two

Gradually, work at the office settled down following the murder inquiry and life began to return to something like normal. Well, as normal as the usual chaos associated with inner-city policing can be. The following Wednesday, I was on late cover and returned to Lawrence Road to sign off just after one in the morning. I was chatting with the two night-duty detectives when I was called to the telephone. Sighing, and inwardly cursing that I had not gone home earlier, I made my way to the desk.

'Hello, sir, this is the Force Control Room. Can you make Hope Street as soon as possible. A police officer has been shot.'

All thoughts of home vanished and, together with some of the lads, I headed for Hope Street, at the time the police headquarters. A large rambling building, it had originally been the Liverpool School for the Blind. An inquiry office, manned twenty-four hours a day, faced out on to the Philharmonic Hall, home to the world-famous Liverpool orchestra. Although the station was within easy walking distance of the bustling city night life, it was a relatively quiet area. On arrival, I was briefed by Nat Sheron who was running the inquiry.

Just after midnight, the driver of a marked police vehicle had stopped a Morris Marina car which failed to heed the red traffic lights at the nearby junction with Hardman Street. Three men were in the vehicle and, without warning, a shot was fired at the officer as he approached. Thankfully, this missed him. The incident was witnessed by Sergeant Nick Doran from behind his desk in the foyer of the police building. He ran out to assist and another shot was fired. Sergeant Doran fell, mercifully only slightly injured. The Marina roared off in the direction of Liverpool cathedral. The frantic call from the officers at the scene caused an immediate and massive response. Road blocks were set up throughout the city and every available officer was summoned to the scene. By now there was reason to believe that the three men may have been involved in another shooting incident earlier that night in Manchester.

Nat's theory was that they would not have gone far in the car, so a street-by-street search was begun in the immediate area. I was one of only two officers present who were authorised to carry firearms. I buckled on the shoulder holster and checked my Smith and Wesson .38 Police Special, reflecting as I always did on how much I disliked guns. I had long ago lost count of how many times I had been armed but the distaste did not go away. The knowledge that I held the means of death in the cold steel in my hand made me very aware of my mortality. Not only that, when you carried a firearm, your own life and those of your colleagues could well depend on how you reacted to any given situation. The training was intense and the failure rate high, but only in a real situation would you discover how you responded. A very old friend of mine Detective Sergeant George Penny was my partner and driver.

We were directed to hit all the clubs in the immediate area in case the gunmen were mingling with the customers. We encountered no problems when we explained the reason for our unusual visits, all the managers co-operated fully. Mind you, with one of our own being shot, any objection would have been short-lived!

A radio call summoned us to an entry off nearby Catherine Street where uniformed officers had found the suspect Marina. It appeared to have been abandoned and we checked it visually with guns drawn. There was a fear that it may be booby-trapped, so our brief was to ascertain there were no occupants. This was not simple as it sounds. It entailed us approaching the vehicle down a long dark alleyway. Taking advantage of the sparse protection, we inched along, covering each other as we scampered a few feet at a time. Having determined that no one was in the car, we immediately moved back, in case of explosion.

Nat's theory that the offenders were still in the vicinity looked a distinct possibility. His concern now was that a householder may have been taken hostage. With this in mind, he decided to search premises in the immediate neighbourhood. This was an extensive operation. Residents were awoken, house by house, and the situation was explained to them before their homes were methodically checked. George and I were present at each address in case our firepower was required. It was a slow, laborious job, and as we were reaching the end of one terrace, Nat ordered that we stop at the last house by the junction. We were then instructed to return to HQ for a debriefing, as officers who had enjoyed a night's sleep were on their way to relieve us.

We strolled back through the grounds of Liverpool cathedral. It was a beautiful morning and I found it hard to believe that potentially fatal violence had taken place only a short while earlier in such historic surroundings. We cheeked in our firearms and George scampered off to grab us a coffee. My mouth was parched, undoubtedly from the tension I had felt over the last few hours. Despite this, I was pleased that my hand had not trembled as I handed the gun over.

'Mike,' George asked me as we sipped our drink, 'it's not the same as shooting at targets on the range, is it?'

'Not really, why?'

'Well, the law of averages means we will have to use them for real sometime.'

I found that an unwelcome and sobering thought.

An officer from the Special Branch strolled over and engaged us in conversation. He was well rested and fresh, having just been called in. During our chat we told him all that we knew and I was intrigued to watch him circulate, talking only to officers who had been on all night. I drew this to George's attention and, as time elapsed, we were fascinated by the change that came over him. First his jacket came off, then he ruffled his hair and pulled down his tie and undid the top button of his shirt.

We only realised what he was up to when he approached senior officers who were attending for the first time, and began to brief them on the events as they had unfolded. Without actually saying so, his knowledge and generally dishevelled state gave the impression that he had been on all night! Politics, I suppose.

It was almost lunchtime by the time I got home, having worked nearly thirty hours in all. The adrenaline was still pumping and I knew that, until I relaxed, sleep would be impossible. With yet another cup of coffee I sat in my garden, Fluffy, my cat, on my knee. As I stroked him and he responded with his magnificent purr, I felt the tension receding.

The inquiry into the shooting continued and was now under the control of the Special Branch. The following morning I was due to start a trial at the Crown Court, so I had played my last part in the investigation. On my arrival at St George's Hall I was told some devastating news.

Just after dawn, a large squad of armed police officers had raided a house in Oxford Road, Waterloo, in the north end of the city. They were seeking to arrest three men in connection with the shooting of Sergeant Doran. The officers made their way to the first floor to be met with a hail of bullets and a sergeant fell seriously wounded. He was dragged to safety and rushed to Walton Hospital where he underwent an emergency operation for stomach wounds.

The gunfire was returned by the police and, after some three-quarters of an hour, the three occupants surrendered. They were taken into custody and firearms and large quantities of explosives, including gelignite, were recovered. So potentially dangerous was some of the haul that residents in the road were evacuated while Army Bomb Disposal teams examined and removed the items. The sergeant later made as full a recovery as could be expected and went on to serve for many more years.

George rang me later in the day to see if I had heard the news. We arranged to meet for a drink later that night at the bar in HQ. As we were talking, an inspector from the Branch joined us. The first words he said brought it home to both of us.

'You were lucky, weren't you, Mike?'

'How do you mean?'

'After Nick was shot you were searching the houses in Huskisson Street, yeah?'

'Yes, but nothing happened.'

'They were watching you from a bedroom window. They'd got into a house while they waited for the hunt to finish. If you hadn't been stood down you'd have met them. They were in the next block you were due to search.'

George and I were very quiet for the remainder of the night as we privately reflected on what might have been.

Chapter Twenty-Three

The following morning, Tom Whittlestone and Gordon McKenzie held a press conference at HQ, speaking to an assembled horde of the media desperate for news of the incident in Waterloo. Halfway through the briefing they were called out from the room. Once again, guns were on the streets.

As the conference was taking place, it was a normal morning in the jeweller's premises O'Hares, in Breck Road, Anfield. One of the assistants, 56-year-old Alfred, a father of seven, had told his colleagues he was looking forward to a party the following day to mark his son's engagement. That particular day he was only working due to the absence of another staff member. Without warning, a gang of men dressed in overalls, their faces concealed behind balaclavas, rushed in brandishing sawn-off shotguns. With great courage Alfred tried to confront the robbers. He was callously gunned down with a shotgun blast to his chest. As he slumped, dying, to the floor the raiders fled empty-handed and escaped in a stolen car. A passing motorist tried to stop them but they evaded him.

A massive inquiry began into this brutal attack and detectives were drafted into the investigation from every division. The public were shocked by the callousness of such a cold-blooded slaying and there was real fear that the gang could well strike again. We put ourselves about and addresses all over the city were hit in the man-hunt. We put tremendous pressure on the street to arrest these killers. It was most definitely bad for business as far as professional criminals were concerned.

Driven by the senseless slaughter of an innocent man a prodigious effort was put into the job. After a meticulous inquiry, arrests were made and firearms were recovered. One of those arrested lived in Runcorn in Cheshire and sawn-off shotguns and a large quantity of cartridges were found concealed in a false panel in a shed in the garden.

Two men were later sentenced to life imprisonment for the murder. As their fate was announced neither showed any sign of contrition – they just smiled. Other robberies continued and the need for a specialised squad to tackle such ruthless individuals became increasingly apparent.

I was driving home just after midnight and was stationary with the lights against me at the end of Upper Parliament Street when I saw, crossing in front of my vehicle, a man who was circulated as being wanted in connection with a wounding outside a local pub. I jumped out of my car and, after some initial protest, nicked him. Although there were a lot of people milling about, no one interfered with the arrest. As I was putting him into the car another vehicle drove up alongside. Four young men got out and it was only too obvious they meant to get involved. Fortunately I knew the driver and, with a few choice words of advice, they backed off and drove away. I took my prisoner to the Main Bridewell and lodged him there.

As I sat in a back room completing my paperwork I could not help but smile when I heard two young uniformed officers telling a sergeant the details of an arrest they had just made. Their prisoner was a happy drunk, swaying and smiling as he held on to the charge counter for support. They had found him on his hands and knees on a pedestrian crossing on busy Lime Street, in danger of being run over. He was asked what he was doing and had explained he was trying to roll up the black and white carpet to take home to his wife as a present!

Returning to my interrupted journey home, something was niggling at the back of my mind about the driver of the car who had stuck his nose in to my arrest. As I drove out of the tunnel it suddenly hit me. He was on bail to Mike for a street robbery in Granby Street in Toxteth. Some weeks earlier, with two others, he had attacked a man and stolen his money. He had been nicked but was on bail with a curfew. He was not supposed to be out of his house between 9 p.m. and 7 a.m. so he was in breach of his bail conditions!

First thing the next day, I rang Mike and filled him in on what had happened. Mike pulled the offender later that morning and he was so shocked he admitted a robbery he had committed while he was on bail. Because he had not only breached his bail but had also committed offences during it, he was kept in custody for some weeks before his case was disposed of at the Crown Court.

*

Later one evening I was making inquiries into an arson attack on a flat in the Smithdown Road area. Some maniac had drenched the front door with petrol and ignited it. Fortunately the family had managed to escape with their two young children. The following day, with Detective Constables Dave Bray and Sid Wardale, I was calling at homes in the vicinity in an effort to track any witnesses. One door was opened by a young woman. Having confirmed that she had not seen anything until the arrival of the fire service, I mentioned that we had got no response from calls to the neighbouring flat.

'That's Helen. I don't think she was in, she must have had a date.'

'Well, we will have to call back unless you know for certain she was out.'

'She must have been. She was showing me a new pair of knickers she'd bought yesterday.'

'I'm sorry. I don't make the connection.'

'She must have had a date with a new feller last night.'

'Did she tell you that?'

'Not in so many words, but why else would she have bought herself new knickers?'

Silly of me not to have realised that myself.

Within a few days we had made an arrest for the arson. It had been committed by a local man who had had a minor row with the husband of the house. He had seethed over this before committing such a stupid, yet potentially fatal, crime. It was eventually to cost him several years of his liberty.

Chapter Twenty-Four

Armed robbery was still a force-wide problem and I had long ago lost count of the number that I had helped to investigate. Even the ones that scarcely rated a passing mention in the press affected the victims badly. In some cases those who had looked down the barrel of a firearm, been pistol-whipped or threatened with knives and clubs, never totally recovered from their ordeal. I totally disagreed with the opinion that the offenders were hard men. Anyone can be tough when threatening unarmed civilians with a gun. It was a fact of life that the rewards for such actions could be extremely fruitful.

On 30th October 1975 probably one of the most professional gangs ever encountered in Liverpool struck on my patch. Tony was on holiday and I was performing acting-superintendent duties in his absence. I arrived at Allerton station in the morning and updated myself with the overnight crime. I told the clerk I was going for a coffee to the canteen before I tackled the morning paperwork. I returned to the office a few minutes later, carrying my drink, and heard the clerk say to a caller on the phone. 'Here's Mr Mulloy now, sir. He will tell you all about it.'

The caller turned out to be Gordon McKenzie who

was asking about an armed robbery at a British Rail depot that had been reported within the last few minutes. As I was not clairvoyant, I didn't have any idea of what he was talking about. I told him I would deal with it. Not surprisingly, I asked the clerk how I was supposed to know about this. His lame excuse was that as he had no knowledge he did not wish to appear ignorant!

Obviously, he was not too concerned if I did.

Just after 9.30 that morning a Securicor armoured security vehicle had driven into the British Rail depot in Combermere Street carrying staff wages. The driver alighted, carrying four bags containing over £26,000. He entered the main office building, heading towards the wages office. As he reached the main foyer he was confronted by three armed masked men. He had a gun jabbed into his face and was told he would be 'blasted' by the other men, who were carrying sawn-off shotguns. Courageously, the driver tried to fight but was struck and the bags were snatched. As the robbers fled across the yard they were watched by workmen and office staff and a warning shot was discharged before they made good their escape. The discharge of such a weapon sounds like a clap of thunder. It also illustrated that these guys were not bluffing – their firearms were loaded and they were quite prepared to use them. One can only speculate how they might react if they were cornered by unarmed officers. These were dangerous men.

I made my way to the scene and began to co-ordinate the inquiry. From the outset I recognised that this was a meticulously planned raid which bore all the hallmarks of experienced and ruthless robbers. Initially we discovered that three men were seen to drive a Ford Cortina into an adjacent yard shortly before the attack. They had commandeered decorators' ladders to scale a ten-foot wall which was only feet from the building in which they had carried out the ambush, but which completely concealed the getaway car. The yard was ideal for their purposes as, from there, they could make a quick exit with a wide-open run to the main road. Within a few minutes' drive they would have been onto the motorway system.

Road blocks were set up throughout Merseyside and a street-by-street search was made for the bandits' vehicle. We had long ago learnt that this was likely to be stolen and abandoned within a short distance of the scene. We were not disappointed. Within half an hour the vehicle was discovered in nearby Dorothy Street and I flooded the area with officers. The men had been seen running down an entry into Janet Street and there they had vanished.

The Cortina had been stolen from the Speke area the day before the robbery, and had been painted and fitted with false number plates which related to a genuine car of the same make and model. Although this vehicle was to take us no further, the sighting of another car looked more promising. The officers who had trawled Janet Street came up with the number of another Cortina. Several people had heard what sounded like a gunshot and their attention had been drawn to the car as it had been driven away by three men. More importantly, two had noted down the registration number which they passed on to the detectives.

A Major Incident Control had been set up at

Lawrence Road and inquiries revealed that the second Cortina was registered to a man called David Martin, whose current address was in Harlow in Essex. Initially this was a blow. Because of the distance involved, it was at first assumed that it was another car bearing a false plate or that the number had been recorded wrongly. Officers from Essex visited the address on our behalf but got no positive result. Martin had left his wife and family some months earlier and although he was in regular contact, his own address was not known to them.

Some days later, Martin called of his own volition into Borehamwood Police Station just outside London. He was interviewed by Metropolitan officers and he explained that he had indeed owned this vehicle, but had disposed of it several days before the robbery in Liverpool. Some months earlier he had bought it from the mother of a man called Alex Peters, who had loaned him £500 towards the purchase price. Having been unable to meet the financial payments because of the split from his family, Martin had eventually agreed to return the car to Peters. The deal was that Peters, who lived in Ramsgate in Kent, would sell the car to recoup his loan and anything outstanding would go to Martin.

At our request Kent officers interviewed Peters who agreed completely with this version of events and said he was still in possession of the car. He confirmed that it had been returned days before the robbery and had not been out of the area. Both men made written witness statements relating to the vehicle. The officers who had conducted the interviews on our behalf seemed satisfied, as this version of events was supported by other people.

We had already been active with informants in

relation to this blag. Word on the streets was that outsiders from the city were definitely involved. There was something I was not happy about but I could not put my finger on it. At my request, both Peters and Martin were detained in the respective police areas. Long before dawn, accompanied by Roy Horton, Ray Murray and Dave Monteith, I began the long journey down south by car.

We made good time until we hit London and, having crawled through the traffic, we arrived at Borehamwood Station, near Elstree Film Studios. We told the officer on the desk who we were and spent over half an hour kicking our heels in the foyer. Just as I was getting impatient, a sergeant came to us and took us to the office of his inspector. At first his demeanour was cool but changed completely when he realised who we were: 'Bloody hell, you're from Liverpool! We thought you were rubber heels coming to turn us over!'

It appeared that he had been warned of four unknown men arriving, wearing suits and carrying brief-cases, and had responded in the belief that we were part of the Met's discipline department. A frantic tidying of the office had taken place to ensure everything was in order, which was why we had been delayed. Having sorted out the misunderstanding, we got straight down to business.

Martin was a large dark-haired man in his early twenties and although nervous, he repeated his story of the purchase of the car. We had turned his flat over and recovered the registration document which showed him as being the keeper of the vehicle. We took him to Ramsgate with us, where Alex Peters was being detained and there we saw the Cortina in the police yard. Peters positively identified the vehicle as being the one in question but new factors were now at the front of my mind. The registration plates were one digit in error from the log book and the car reeked of thinners. Even to the naked eye it had obviously been thoroughly cleaned inside and out.

Roy and I interviewed Peters but he was adamant that the vehicle had not left the premises where it was being worked on. If he was to be believed, on the day of the robbery not only was this car in Kent but it was in no condition to be driven as it had no rear axle. Our inquiries continued and, with Ray, I visited the garage where the work had allegedly been carried out. The garage owner made a show of checking through his records and eventually produced documentation to this effect.

This was just too good to be true. Was it just sheer coincidence it could be so emphatically proven this vehicle could never have been in Liverpool? Ray and I went with our instincts and really got into the proprietor of the garage. We put it straight on the line so that he was under no illusion where we were coming from. I had formed the impression that these people thought they were dealing with plods from the sticks, so we quickly dispelled any such impression.

Once the garage owner fully understood the serious-ness of the situation he realised which side of the line he should stand. He was a friend of Peters, who had told him some story about the car possibly being involved in a road accident. He had agreed to go along with the tale about the axle although, in fact, he had not carried out any repairs on the vehicle at all. Now we were getting somewhere. Faced with this back at Ramsgate nick, Peters gave it up. He was adamant he had played no part in the robbery but gave us his version of events. John Morris and Dave Wright, two men from Nottingham, had visited him the day before the blag and had hired the car for cash. When they had returned it the next day he had become suspicious and had concocted this elaborate story. He had cleaned the car and replaced the number plates as, when the vehicle was returned, it was bearing a different registration mark. He was adamant he knew nothing of our blag.

The whole charade was now collapsing in on itself. Dave and I interviewed Martin again and he too folded like a pack of cards. It turned out that he had never seen the vehicle in his life. Some months earlier, Morris had approached him and asked him to register the car in his name. Obviously plans were even then in progress to commit the armed robbery. Martin had done so and, after the robbery, Morris, Peters and Wright had called to see him in London. He was told the car had been involved in an accident and he had gone along with the cover story. Even now, we did not have the full truth but lengthy interviews got it all out of them. Eventually, both Martin and Peters admitted that they were aware that a robbery had occurred and Morris went into specific detail about it.

We arrested the pair of them and, by the time the paperwork was completed, it was after one in the morning. We had been on continuous duty for some twenty-two hours without even a meal break!

The following morning we began our journey back. I

had arranged for Ian Stewart to travel to Nottingham to arrest Dave Wright, who denied all knowledge of the affair. Back in Liverpool, Roy and I interviewed him, armed with what we already knew, and he soon cracked. He agreed that, on the night of the blag, Morris had called at his home and he had agreed to accompany him to Ramsgate to meet Peters. He was told that the purpose of the trip was to arrange a cover story for the robbery. He agreed that the three of them had travelled to London to see Martin and then he and Morris were driven back to Nottingham by Peters. The following Sunday, he had driven Morris to Porthcawl in South Wales where he had dropped him off. Now we were getting somewhere. We had three men in custody who had assisted in a cover-up but we still did not have the gunmen.

Chapter Twenty-Five

The net was slowly closing in. Our inquiries had yielded three suspects for being the actual blaggers. From the outset we had believed this to be a very professional attack, meticulous and well planned. Now we were informed that several men had come together while serving sentences in Hull Prison for serious crime. As they talked they realised that their downfall had been due to police local knowledge so, in the future, they planned to commit robberies throughout the country. Cars were to be stolen to order and at least one gang member would live well outside the area. It would be this man's eventual responsibility to dispose of any clothing so as to frustrate forensic examination and to conceal the firearms and stolen cash. As a consequence any searches the local police undertook would be fruitless, as they would be carried out hundreds of miles from where the gear had been hidden.

Morris was a handsome man in his thirties, charming and ruthless. He had already served many years imprisonment for armed robbery and was now in the frame for this job. We knew he had been in the Porthcawl area and inquiries started there. The other two were much closer to home. Eddie Dwyer was also in his thirties and of a similar type to Morris but without the charm. At this time he was on bail for a firearm incident in the city centre and his whole background revealed him to be a dangerous and unstable man. According to our sources, he was the only one not trusted to have access to their gang's arsenal of weapons as he was capable of using them to settle an argument of his own. The third man, Jim Turner, was a close associate of Dwyer's and well respected in the same circles. Now the time had come to try and take all three off the streets.

Just after 7a.m. I led a team of armed officers to an address in Toxtoth and, on gaining access, arrested Dwyer. He denied all knowledge of the robbery and gave his wife and family as his alibi. Roy and I interviewed him at Lawrence Road and he persistently denied knowing any of those already in custody, or Morris. I pointed out that it was strange he could not recall Morris as I believed they had both served a prison sentence in the same establishment.

'I was wondering about that. All right, I know him, but you can't pin that job on me just because I know him, can you?'

He agreed that he had seen Morris some weeks earlier but emphatically denied having stayed with him in Porthcawl and, naturally, knew nothing about our robbery. After a lengthy interview he was left alone while we continued our inquiries.

Some time later Roy and I again saw him and this time we found him in a different mood. In the initial interview he had bellowed his replies at us in a vain attempt to intimidate us. Now he was far more reasonable. He had had time to think things over and, of course, was not aware of what sort of hand we held.

'It looks bad to you, it would to me, but I did go to see him at Porthcawl.'

'Why have you repeatedly told lies?'

'They'll throw the key away over this job.'

'What do you mean?'

'You know what I mean. I can't admit being there, it's too heavy a blag. I'll have taking the Cortina that was used from Speke but not being on the blag itself.'

'Where did you take the car from?'

'I'm telling you straight now. This carries fifteen years, so I'll have taking the car and painting the roof white and the rest but I'm not putting myself in the depot. I can't, it's too heavy.'

He would go no further nor would he make a written statement, but agreed to go on an identification parade. Later that evening this was held at the Main Bridewell and we got a result when he was positively identified as being one of the robbery team. He was taken back to Lawrence Road and, on arrival, he spoke to Roy and me.

'Look, I want to trade. What's in it for me if I help you?'

'How d'you mean "trade"?'

'You know I was there but I was only the lookout man. I never fired any gun. It's worth something, isn't it?'

Now we were at least progressing, inasmuch he had admitted being a lookout man on the blag.

'What's that worth?'

'A lesser charge, if I help you get the shooters and the cash.'

There was no way we would consider any deal and, despite further offers, he was later charged and kept in custody, while the hunt for the others went on.

Turner was now on the run. He had heard of our interest in him and had been fortunate to have a very lucky escape. Unbeknown to us, the gang had hired a car from a local rental firm and parked it as a back-up in yet another location during the blag. As it had not been returned, it had been reported stolen to the local police. Their inquiries revealed that it had been hired by someone using a stolen driving licence. Incredibly, despite the haul of many thousands of pounds from the robbery, Turner was greedy enough to return the car some days later! When he was arrested by two local detectives he thought very fast on his feet. He admitted a non-existent theft from the docks while using the vehicle and offered to turn them up some valuable information on other serious crimes. He was given bail later that day and promptly vanished. Reliable sources told us he had flown to America using a false passport. Despite extensive inquiries he was never traced.

Meanwhile, we concentrated on the Porthcawl area in our search for Morris and, days later, we had a break. We obtained a telephone number which he had given to a contact and this was traced to a hotel in the town centre. Local police set up a 24-hour observation operation by armed officers. Late in the afternoon of 27th November he was seen to leave the hotel. He was tackled, brought to the ground and arrested. Within an hour of receiving the news I was off on what was to be an eventful journey to South Wales with Ray and Dave. The following morning we confronted Morris in the cell complex. He was confident and assured and displayed no sign of nerves.

'Who's the detective in charge of the case?'

'I'm Detective Inspector Mulloy. After you've eaten breakfast we're taking you back to Liverpool for further interviews with regard to the armed robbery you are in custody for.'

'OK. I'll talk to you about it later.'

Just after noon we began the drive back in atrocious weather of heavy snow and sleet. We stopped for a meal at a service station and visited the toilets. Dave was handcuffed to Morris and, to spare him embarrassment, he had draped his raincoat over their cuffed wrists. The toilets were busy and, as we were leaving, Ray said in a loud voice, 'Damned disgusting. I don't care what they do in private but there are limits.'

Other customers looked over to see what he was talking about and all eyes rested on Dave and Morris. As they stood facing the urinals, for all the world they appeared to be holding hands. If a furious Dave could have got hold of Ray, as he braved the tuts of disapproval, I dread to think what may have happened!

We continued the journey in very bad weather and, as we went over the brow of a hill, in the distance we could see that there had been a serious accident on the carriageway ahead. Vehicles were alight and the ominous sign of blanket-draped figures on the hard shoulder told the story. As we slowed down to a crawl, a clown driving far too close rammed the rear of our car, which sustained slight damage. I got out to speak to him and he tried to bluster that it was our fault! I flashed my warrant card and he promptly changed his mind, admitting full responsibility.

In such an event, an accident involving a police vehicle should be reported immediately. There were officers about but, because of the carnage, they more than had their hands full. I exchanged details with the other driver and we continued our journey. When I later submitted the report of the damage I received a rap over the knuckles for not reporting it at the scene! Ah, the wisdom of the desk-bound man.

Morris was given a night's rest and his interviews commenced the following morning. He had recently married a local beauty queen and this, plus the sentence he was facing, eventually got him talking. He was already aware of those we had in custody but had no way of knowing what they had said.

After the initial interview he cracked.

'I want to get this sorted out. I never planned the job.'

'Go on.'

'A week before it came off I got a telephone call from Liverpool asking if I was interested. I said yes and they said it was a good one.'

He gave us extensive details about the background planning of the blag and the movements of the gang leading to the attack.

'What happened then?'

'We got there and they had the guns and stuff. I drove the car into the yard and, when the security van came, we did the blag.'

Over lengthy interviews he gave us a chilling insight into the activities of armed robbers. As they had made good their escape there had been an accident. One of the shotguns had been banged against a wall in the entry in their haste. It had discharged and injured Turner in the leg.

'Are you certain about that?'

'Yes, the guns were cocked on the job.'

This revealed that they were not being carried for ornamentation. Why else would they be cocked if not in preparation for discharge? Morris described how they fled in separate cars, meeting up later by Liverpool cathedral. They had been listening in to police transmissions and were aware the car number may have been taken, which caused the cover-up to take place in London and Ramsgate. The outer clothing worn on the job had been burnt and, he added, underneath he was wearing a smart suit and tie. This was so that he could blend into the background as a businessman. After he had made a written statement under caution, he was later charged with robbery and remanded in custody.

The investigation continued and vital intelligence was gathered from a number of sources regarding a large number of other robberies. These included attacks on security vehicles, building societies and business premises in Liverpool, Manchester, Lancashire, Derbyshire, Nottingham and North Wales. The supply and movement of firearms along with the provision and storage of vehicles used on these robberies were tracked over a period of time.

Some weeks later with Jock Stewart, I had a further

interview with Morris. I sensed that he believed that some sort of rapport existed between us. He could not have been further from the truth. I knew that I was dealing with a ruthless thug, no matter the veneer of friendliness and co-operation. Morris was only trying to help himself. He had been quite prepared to terrorise and injure persons to obtain his ends. At no stage did he ever show a flicker of remorse for the victims. The only regret that I ever heard him express was regarding his overnight bag. He complained that they had been so thorough in burning property that could possibly connect them to the Liverpool robbery, his overnight bag was also disposed of.

Towards the end of the interviews he surprised me by a comment he made. 'You'd better watch your back, Mr Mulloy, you've upset certain people.'

'Who's that then?'

'I can't say, but word has it inside that certain people want you out the way. You've upset some bad men.'

In some ways I took it as a compliment. Several armed robbers had made complaints against me in the past in an effort to affect my inquiries, but to no avail. It came with the territory. Robbers would allege anything in an effort to make some mud stick. Popular at this time among robbers who had been convicted and sentenced to lengthy prison terms was the ploy of appearing as a witness for the defence in another case. They would then allege that they had committed the offence being tried before the court. The idea was to cause confusion to the jury and they had little to fear as they were already serving a sentence. It became a farce when, in one of my trials, the 'witness' was six foot tall while the accused was five foot six!

Joking aside, little did I know that Morris's words were to prove prophetic.

Chapter Twenty-Six

The trial of the five men took place before His Honour Judge Nance at Liverpool Crown Court. Dwyer pleaded not guilty to the substantive charge of robbery but Morris accepted his guilt. Peters, Martin and Wright pleaded not guilty to assisting offenders who had committed the crime. The trial lasted for three weeks and was hard fought. I spent over three days in the witness box. Like my officers, I was the subject of sustained, hostile cross-examination and the target of many allegations of malpractice. At the conclusion of proceedings on the second day of my evidence, I glanced at my watch and reasoned that if I got a move on I could make home, have a bath and something to eat before returning as late cover officer. As I was leaving the tunnel, I admit I did rather carve another car up. Although I am normally a patient driver, the Rover in front of me was dawdling away. I accelerated and overtook him where I should not have really done so. I glanced across, and with horror spotted the driver – it was only bloody Judge Nance glaring at me! I shuffled down in my seat and sped away hoping that he had not recognised me.

The following morning I resumed my evidence and

all went well until I was being examined about the accident we had become involved in during our return from Porthcawl. At this stage, Judge Nance indicated that he wished to ask me a question.

'Tell me, Detective Inspector Mulloy, were you the driver of the vehicle?'

'No, sir. The driver was Detective Constable Murray.'

'How very fortunate for all concerned. Carry on, Mr Wolff.'

Mike Wolff, who was defending Dwyer, along with all the other counsels, looked baffled by the comment. Only two people in that room knew what he had meant!

At the end of one day I was talking to Mr Rose, QC, who was representing the Crown when Dwyer beckoned to me from the dock. I stepped forward and asked him what he wanted.

'Mr Mulloy, why are you taking this case so personally?'

If he had seen or cared about the effect of his actions on the terrified office workers and security guards, he would have realised the stupidity of such a question. I had obviously got under his skin. Good, I could live with that.

As the hearing entered the third week, an unusual event occurred. Alongside the court buildings the loop line for the underground railway was nearing completion and the site was a hive of activity. I received a call for an urgent meet with a contact of mine and, that lunchtime, I saw him in the lounge bar of the Legs of Man pub in Lime Street.

'Mike, they're going to spring them. This is dead straight. The idea is to mingle with the workers next door and, when they get the chance, hit the court with shooters and get them out!'

He was unable to say who 'they' were but he was very concerned and was a contact who had always been 100 per cent accurate. Promising to find out what he could, he left me to my thoughts. I was still undecided when I arrived back at the court but any doubts I had were soon dispelled. Tom Whittlestone had received identical information from another source so this had to be taken seriously. A hasty meeting was held and it was decided that I and several other officers in plain clothes would be armed during the remainder of the case. Two days later we stopped and searched two well-known men with convictions for carrying firearms as they attempted to enter the court. We made no secret of the fact that we were armed and, as a result, they must have realised they were on a hiding to nothing and no rescue attempt was ever made.

A lighter moment occurred when it was heard that the jury were to return. At major trials it is not un-common to have members of the public attend just to observe and follow the case throughout its entirety. One couple in their early thirties had been there from day one. They had not missed a second and, although we had never spoken, by now I was on nodding terms with them. They were now being told that, owing to lack of space, they could not be allowed into the court to hear the verdicts. A constable was giving them this informa-tion and I took him to one side and had a word in his ear. When he heard what I had to say, he ushered them through into the area normally reserved for police officers so that they could hear the outcome. Instead of a nod, I received grateful smiles.

The jury returned with unanimous verdicts of guilty in respect of all of the defendants. By now Dwyer was already serving five years for a firearms offence and he received a further fifteen years to be served consecutively. Morris got fourteen years and the other three between six and nine months. These were heavy sentences which not only reflected the serious nature of the crime but the abhorrence felt for those who were prepared to commit them. They had gambled for high stakes and they had lost.

When the sentences were announced there was uproar in the public sector of the court. Morris's wife broke down in tears, screaming at the judge: 'Why don't you strangle him and save the expense?'

One of the ushers whispered to me: 'She has a point there!'

Mike and I were having a drink for old time's sake in the Noah's Ark in Speke one night when two pints were sent over to us. This pub was known locally as the zoo because of all the animals that drink there! I asked the barmaid who the drinks were from and she indicated a guy at the end of the bar – Johnny, a well-known thief whom we had nicked many times. We called him a hardy annual as we pulled him at least once a year. He'd do his time then go right back to petty thieving. He was the sort who couldn't cross the road without thinking of pinching the cat's-eyes. There was a story behind his generosity.

Several years earlier, we had been requested to attend Widnes Magistrates' Courts in Cheshire. Johnny had been arrested on a charge of 'reputed thief loitering', and part of the prosecution case was to prove his last conviction. I was called into the witness box and told the magistrates that I had been present in court on the last occasion he had been convicted of a minor theft. Johnny was then asked if he wished to question me. Indeed he did.

'Mr Mulloy, you have arrested me many times, right?'

'Yes, I suppose so.'

'For wounding, right?'

'Yes.'

'Taking and driving away cars?'

'Yes.'

'Criminal damage?'

'Yes.'

'So I'm not just a thief, I do other things, right?'

Heaven knows how this was supposed to help him, as he promptly got three months. He signalled to us to see him underground in the cell complex. When we did so, he thanked us profusely for coming to court to try and help him. Somehow he had got it in his mind that we had given evidence on his behalf! Ever since then, if he saw us he sent a pint over and regaled everyone who would listen that we were the best coppers he'd ever had dealings with.

On Christmas Eve I was aroused from sleep yet again. A body had been found in suspicious circumstances in a side street off Upper Parliament Street in Toxteth and my presence was required. The body was that of a middle-aged man who was lying on his back on the footwalk. What had caused the attending officers concern was a deep gash on the back of his head. The area had a reputation of being plagued by muggers and the fear was that he had fallen victim to an attack, with fatal consequences.

Having examined the dead man, I searched his pockets and from inside his jacket I retrieved a wallet stuffed with money. The contents also revealed that he lived in the locality so I sent two detectives to his address. A minute scan of the scene revealed skin and blood on a low wall, adjacent to the body. I was of the opinion that he had collapsed, struck his head as he fell and died there. This was borne out by the officers who had called at his home. He had gone out for a walk after complaining of chest pains, so all the signs were that the poor man had suffered a heart attack.

By the time inquiries were complete I had given up hope of any more sleep. I did not enjoy the traditional Christmas Eve celebrations that lunch hour, possibly from tiredness, but more likely because I joined them straight from attending the post-mortem examination which had confirmed my theory.

New Year came and it began as the old one had finished. A man walked into Admiral Street station and surrendered himself, stating he had just killed a girl. A search of the grounds of a local church revealed the body of a 27-year-old woman who had been strangled. The story was a depressingly familiar one. She was on the game and had gone to the venue with the man for sexual intercourse. She had angered him by laughing at his lack of prowess and he had simply strangled her. Overcome with guilt, he had walked into the police station and confessed to what he had done.

The murder had not been committed in my division, so normally I would not have been involved. However, her body had to be formally identified and it turned out that I had arrested her some years earlier for receiving stolen property. Once again, I was called out of my bed to make a positive identification at her post-mortem. She was a nice woman, always ready to have a talk and a laugh, and it was a sad end to her short life. She also left behind two small children.

A few days later, Tom Whittlestone phoned me at my office. He told me he was on late cover and arranged for me to see him about nine that night in the bar at HQ. As usual, he gave no reason. It could be to pass on some words of encouragement, more likely it was to give me a rollicking over some misdemeanour. Offhand I could think of no sin I had recently committed but that didn't mean Tom hadn't found out about an old one.

Sharing a drink later that evening, Tom disposed of the small talk and came right to the point.

'You're on the move again, Mike. You did an excellent job with the Robbery Squad. We're now setting up a permanent unit of detectives. I think you're going to enjoy it.'

I sat back to listen to his plans.

Chapter Twenty-Seven

Violent birth of a top police squad!

That was the *Liverpool Echo*'s banner headline announcing the establishment of the Serious Crime Squad. The article which followed gave the background to our formation and highlighted the infamous summer's day when all hell had broken loose in Liverpool. The shooting of the police officers, followed by the callous slaying of an innocent man was the reason we had been set up. It was intended that we would take the killers and gunmen head-on. The unit consisted of four teams of two detective sergeants and four detective constables, each under an inspector; the overall commander was a detective chief inspector. The suits and ties of a divisional detective were replaced by jeans and sweatshirts, the uniform of the streets. For all of the founder members it was a new concept in policing.

We were to be called in to assist local divisions with major inquiries but wherever possible the final responsibility would remain with them. This meant we could be flexible and available to help out wherever we were needed. We would also be the nucleus in future of all major murder inquiries. In our own right we would be making investigations into major criminal figures which were bound to bring us up against armed robbers. The braggers knew no divisional boundaries and now, neither, did we. We were soon housed in a brand new police station at Walton Lane and the first few weeks were spent settling in and getting to know our new teams. We had sectored the force area and I had responsibility for the south end of the city, including Toxteth and the Wirral area where I lived. We were not to wait long before we had our first murder inquiry.

Within two weeks we were drafted into the city centre to join the hunt for the killer of 73-year-old Thomas, a harmless old man with deep spiritual beliefs, who had lived in his flat on the ground floor of a Victorian building on Huskisson Street for over twenty years. Now he had been discovered dead in the hallway with stab wounds. The suspicion that he had been the target of a mugging was reinforced when two other victims were traced who had been attacked in the area at about the same time. One man was extremely fortunate to have survived. The 52-year-old had been attacked and stabbed several times in the chest and abdomen as he was robbed in the street. He had managed to stagger to a block of flats and had collapsed in an alcove where he lay for nine hours before being found and rushed to hospital. The other victim, another elderly man, had been punched and had a knife jabbed into his throat as he was robbed. The two survivors both gave similar descriptions of the lone robber – this was one dangerous man.

We ran the inquiry from Hope Street and a massive

amount of work went into the case for several weeks. On a number of occasions we followed up promising leads but unfortunately they led nowhere. An arrest was made but the suspect was released because of lack of evidence. As the incidents that needed following up decreased in number we were withdrawn, leaving the inquiry in the hands of the division. It was a disappointing and frustrating start but that's the way it goes sometimes. There are no miracles in solving crime – just hard work, patient enquiry and that little bit of luck that this time evaded us.

Some weeks later, in the early evening, the telephone rang at home and I was called out to another murder, this time on the Wirral. I had a very heavy cold and could well have done with staying at home, but that was out of the question.

Martha, a 75-year-old widow, had been found battered to death in the kitchen of her three-storey, terraced Victorian home in Princess Terrace, just outside Birkenhead town centre. Martha, who lived alone, had suffered extensive injuries to her head.

As I looked about the neat house, now a scene of bloody carnage with the elderly woman lying there, I wondered to myself if I would ever get used to witnessing such sights. She had been battered about the head with a blunt instrument and from the ransacked state of the house, it appeared that the motive was robbery. By chance the doctor who attended at the scene to certify death was my own general practitioner, Dr Hussain from Bebington. At least I got some sympathy from him for my sneezes and snuffles.

My team got stuck in right away and I spoke at length

with Martha's seventeen-year-old grandson who had discovered the body. Having received no reply at the front of the house, he had made his way to the rear and discovered the back door ajar. On entering, he had made his gruesome find and was still badly shaken by his ordeal.

One of my lads, DS Alan McFarlane, was questioning a local man in another room when I was called out to be told he had got a result. The man had cracked and made a full admission to the murder. Within hours we had cleared the matter up, which shows how your fortunes can change within days. The inquiry was now passed on to the division to complete and we were free for the next one – and nobody doubted there would be another one.

As it turned out, the next case was a professional blag. Hooded gunmen had staged a multi-thousand-pound robbery in Toxteth. A security vehicle was being driven along just after nine in the morning when a van swerved in front and a second vehicle blocked them in from behind. Several men armed with shot-guns and baseball bats attacked the security vehicle, shattering the windows. The driver and his mate were dragged from the van, beaten about the head, threatened with the shooters and forced to open the rear doors. After grabbing the money bags, the robbers escaped.

It was a thoroughly planned hit by men who would have brooked no resistance. Both the security men were in hospital being treated for their injuries and we started the hunt right away. Within a short while, both the vehicles used in the raid were found abandoned. They had been hired on stolen driving licences and were brought to Admiral Street station for forensic examination.

Meanwhile a detective sergeant in another part of the city, who had no knowledge of this attack, received a call from an informant. When he later met up with this man what he discovered was dynamite. The informant knew all about our robbery and was able to name those who had committed it. Even better, he was able to house one who was living with a woman well away from his normal address. I was immediately contacted with this information and we began to plan a hit of our own.

The premises we were looking at was on one of the top floors of a notorious block of flats in the city. Our initial surveillance revealed the suspect's car parked up in a nearby side street, so it was looking promising. Normally we would have raided the flat around dawn in an effort to catch the occupants asleep. This gave us a definite advantage, especially when firearms were concerned. However, I decided to hit it right away as there was a good chance of finding some of the stolen cash there. I arranged firearms for myself and several of the team and made a plan of action.

If we could force entry into the flat at the rear and front simultaneously, I figured we had a better chance of taking any occupants out. This meant that some of us would have to climb over the rear railings of the adjoining flats to gain access to the small balcony at the back. I hate heights, but I could not expect others to do it if I wouldn't and Detective Constable Don Jones agreed to accompany me. We made our precarious way onto the landing and whispered into the radio that we were in place. At a given signal we smashed into the flat through the balcony windows and the rest of the team hammered down the front door. We in so fast the guy stood no chance. In bed with his girlfriend, he was caught stark naked with firearms levelled at him on both sides and he gave no resistance as he was arrested. The search of the flat resulted in the recovery of a large amount of cash and a sawn-off shotgun. We were elated. Within hours we had one in the net, but our problems were by no means over.

Our presence had aroused interest and crowds had gathered, both on the landings of the various floors and in the street below. As we eventually made our way out with the robber, we came under attack. We were pelted with missiles and, as we reached the comparative safety of our cars, rocks, bottles and even bins rained down on us. We were in a dangerous situation, unable to extricate ourselves. Hordes of local children, some only toddlers, were put in the roadway to prevent us driving off while the sustained barrage went on. Some people should never be allowed to have kids.

We had to call for assistance and the first uniformed officers to arrive met with a similar attack. Eventually, a unit of the Operational Support Division, an elite public disorder unit, was required to clear the mob. The strange thing was that none of the crowd had the slightest idea, or even cared, what the arrested man had done. Within days, the rest of the robbers were also in custody and later were sentenced to heavy terms of imprisonment.

One of the detectives from the division where the

robbery had occurred could at times come across as a very self-important man. For whatever reason, he had got up my guys' noses and they were looking to get their own back. We stayed at Admiral Street for a few days while the others on the job were mopped up and they got their chance when they discovered that he was constructing a driveway to his home on his day off. The council had quoted rather a high price to do the work and only they were authorised to do the job on the pavement. He had reckoned he could the job himself much cheaper. The lads cruised past a few times and waited until his hard work had nearly completed the task.

One of my lads then telephoned him, identifying himself as being from the council engineers. He explained that several of the detective's neighbours had contacted his department to allege that he was pre- paring unauthorised access to his drive. Naturally, this was met with blustering denials. Ah well, the matter could soon be cleared up by a visit to his home later that afternoon.

Racing back to his home, the lads had hysterics watching him rushing about replacing paving stones he had laboriously removed. They were not satisfied until the whole job was over. He then got another call to say the engineers would not be able to make the site visit after all!

Not to be outdone the divisional lads had a go at him as well. At an evening dinner held in Woolton, he and his wife turned up well after the meal had begun. This was not a surprise as he had been told the function was being held at a hotel in Southport, nearly thirty miles away. Not only that, although everyone else was dressed casually, they had been informed that it was a formal occasion and both were immaculate in evening dress!

Chapter Twenty-Eight

Just after nine o'clock on the morning of Saturday, 31st July 1976, a man was leaving his home for work. On entering the back entry of his home in Toxteth he saw what he first thought was a tailor's dummy lying at the end of the alley. With horror he then realised that it was the body of a young woman. He dashed back into his home and contacted the police and within minutes uniformed officers arrived.

I was on rest day and just about to leave the house with Carol when I was telephoned and told of the incident. I travelled to the scene and joined up with Frank Jones from the division. The woman lay on her back with her knees raised and one arm stretched out above her head. Within a short time we had established that she was Margaret, a 28-year-old mother of two who lived only 500 yards from where she lay. She had remarried just a few weeks earlier and I had the unenviable task of calling at her home address and informing her husband of his loss. He was shattered by the news and so distressed it was a considerable time before he recovered enough to assist us. He accompanied me to Admiral Street to help us with her background and movements and, for security reasons, I left a detective constable at the flat.

We learnt from her husband that she had left their home late the previous night but had not said where she was off to. She had lived in the area for many years and was extremely well known, frequenting the many pubs and clubs in the area. I set up the Murder Control for the incident and general press appeals were issued. Initial medical examination suggested that she had been asphyxiated and had probably died where she had been found.

The first day in a Control is always the most arduous and, just after ten that night, I was at my desk reading statements and noting jobs to be allocated when Frank came in. I brought him up to date and we discussed how we were progressing.

'Come on, Mike, I'll buy you a pint upstairs.'

Rubbing my eyes, I agreed. Since I had not eaten since breakfast I could grab a sandwich as well. We were talking at the bar when someone asked me if I seen the detective constable who I had left at the flat recently.

'No, not since this morning, why?'

Suddenly, it dawned on me – I had forgotten to send anyone to relieve him! A car was hastily sent to collect him and, when he turned up, he was very reasonable about the long wait. Or, should I say, diplomatic?

I had allocated action messages regarding the various licensed premises to the General Enquiry Section and, late one evening, I was reading the recent statements that had flooded in when two of my lads, Dave Monteith and John Hodson, entered the room.

'Boss,' John said, 'we've had a bit of a problem.'

'What's that?'

'You know that club in Dale Street, the one with all the flashing lights outside?'

'Yeah, never been in it but I know the one.'

'We've just been there,' Dave went on, 'and a guy from the club blanked us. Wouldn't even let us speak to the customers, never mind the staff. Point-blank refused to let us show the photo round.'

'Come on,' I said, grabbing my coat. We drove to the club and, on gaining admittance, I spoke with this guy. He told us he could not care less about our inquiry and I found him a most objectionable character, with a bullying, hectoring manner.

'OK, what time does your licence run to?'

'Midnight, why?'

'You'll see.'

With that we left the club and, as the lads dropped me off, I told them to collect me at midnight. I knew full well that he would not close at that time. Although I had never been in his club I had driven past often enough to know he certainly did not stick to those hours. Twenty past twelve saw us again at the door of his club, which was in full swing, music booming out and thronged with customers.

'I told you I'd be back. Close down now, it's past midnight.'

'I'm not telling that drunken lot to go. You'll have to do it, and there's only three of you.'

'Take a look outside, pal.'

He did so and saw two units of the Operational Support Division. I beckoned to them and within minutes the club was vacated and closed. I gave him some harsh advice about co-operation with a murder inquiry and left him to think it over.

The following morning he called at the station, all sweetness and light, a completely different character. He was full of profuse apologies for the misunderstanding and that night the lads went in and did the business.

Any satisfaction I felt was short-lived when I later found that his licence was only to 10 p.m. anyway, so he had had me over for a couple of hours!

The inquiry ran on for some weeks, but further medical examination revealed that in fact Margaret had not been murdered. It was a very unusual event but the inquest eventually recorded a verdict of death by natural causes.

A raid had been carried out at Homepride Bakeries in Walton as the wages were being delivered to the factory early one afternoon. The security guard alighted from the vehicle and, as he was about to enter the building, three men in overalls approached him. Without warning, he was struck a heavy blow to the head with a sawn-off shotgun. He fell to the ground, bloodied and barely conscious. His attackers grabbed the case containing several thousands of pounds and ran to a waiting vehicle, which sped off.

We were called in immediately and, within a short time, we had found the getaway car in nearby Walton Vale. Inquiries showed that this had been a well-planned operation. The overalls had been carefully designed to match those worn by the work staff. We raided several suspects' home before we got the breakthrough we needed, thanks to Detective Constable John Gaffrey.

John was truly one of the nicest people I have ever

known. Tragically, a few years later he died in a car smash on the Wirral just a few days before Christmas, leaving a wife and young family. His death blighted my season and a massive attendance at his funeral from all walks of life showed the affection he had been held in.

John unearthed information about the attack from one of his contacts and later that day we met his informant in the Coffee House pub in Wavertree. The man was able to give us a lot on the job, including some aspects we were not aware of. Armed with this and further background checks, we were ready to strike the following morning.

I led the armed raid on one arrest in Orrell Park in the north of the city and we took a 28-year-old man into custody. He was married with a young family and had no previous convictions. After a lengthy interview he broke down and admitted being the driver of the stolen car used in the raid. He went on to make a written statement and told us that he had been tempted to take part because of the extreme financial difficulties he was facing.

I accepted what he told us and, although I could sympathise with the situation he and his family were now in, I could not forget the guard who had been brutally attacked while going about his job. Within twenty-four hours we also had the other two offenders in custody. The man I had arrested later faced up to his responsibility at the Crown Court and pleaded guilty. He received eight years' imprisonment. His companions denied the charges but were subsequently convicted and received longer terms of imprisonment.

I was now told that, to enhance my experience, I had

been selected to attend the Police Staff College, Bramshill, for a command course which would last fourteen weeks. I did not have the slightest interest in going but, for political reasons, I was aware that I should seem keen to participate – even though I was sure it would be a waste of time. Jack Bird was my boss and over a period of weeks I worked on him, intimating that my absence could cause him a great deal of inconvenience. I was successful inasmuch as that he became convinced it was vital I remain on the squad. 'Leave it to me,' I was told. 'I will sort it out with Mr Whittlestone.'

Later that day I was summoned to Tom's office at HQ. He asked me if I was trying to get off the course. Naturally I strongly denied this, giving the bull expected that it was a unique opportunity and rubbish like that.

'Well, why the hell is Mr Bird so adamant that you can't be spared?'

'I have no idea, sir.'

'You've never suggested that to him, I suppose?'

'As if, sir.'

'As if, sir – I bloody know you. You're trying to work one on him. Well, it won't wash with me. You're going, so leave Jack alone! He has enough to worry about.'

I had tried my best. I also had another slight problem to face. Four days before I was due to attend the course, which was naturally a residential one, Carol and I were moving house. Helped by friends and her mum and dad, Bill and Elsie Casey, we moved in and shortly afterwards I was on the motorway, leaving her surrounded by packing cases.

After I had completed the course, I was duly summoned to see Ken Oxford, the Chief Constable, to discuss my career. He was satisfied by the report regarding my progress and work at the college, and his advice was for me to transfer away from Liverpool to accelerate my prospects of promotion. I did not have the slightest intention of doing any such thing. Why should my valuable local knowledge be wasted? And why should I move Carol away from her family and friends? When I informed him of my views it was apparent that he did not agree with me.

I was glad to shake the dust of this course from my feet and soon settled back into what I was happiest doing. I joined my lads who were trying to catch a man before he killed someone. This maniac was carrying out firebomb attacks in the Northumberland Street area of Toxteth. Although the offences were random, a general pattern was evolving and we could see that he was definitely targeting the elderly. The first attack had occurred in the early hours of the morning some weeks earlier. A petrol bomb had been hurled through the window of a flat occupied by a seventy-year-old woman. Petrol had then been poured through the letter box and ignited. Although the premises were badly damaged in the fire that followed, fortunately the old lady was away in hospital so no one was injured.

Within a short while the arsonist was at work again. In nearby Southwell Place an elderly women was awoken in the early hours by smoke fumes. She lived in a top-floor flat and a petrol-soaked carpet had been placed against her front door and ignited. This was her only escape route. After a frenzied battle with the flames she managed to escape unharmed.

Now he'd struck again. His latest victim was a frail

86-year-old lady who, like the others, lived alone. Just after two in the morning a Molotov cocktail shattered the windows of her bedroom but fortunately she was asleep on the couch in the living room of her ground-floor flat. She managed to grope her way through the flames and dense smoke to her hallway where she became trapped and extremely confused. Alerted by her screams, neighbours forced open the front door and carried her to safety. Her flat was badly damaged in the incident.

This firebomber had to be caught before he killed someone. In the latest incident it was only through good fortune and the bravery of neighbours that a death had been avoided. There was absolutely no doubt that the three attacks were connected and a major inquiry was put into motion to trace the arsonist before he could strike again. The local community were shocked by these events and information flooded in. However, before the investigation was concluded, my section had been called off to assist in a serious robbery elsewhere in the city. Frustratingly this would happen on many occasions. We would initiate an inquiry only to be needed more urgently elsewhere and we would often never find out the result of the inquiry.

The investigation we were called away to attend concerned another team of professional gangsters, this time from out of the city. The Metropolitan Police Flying Squad had received information that some London robbers were planning a job in Liverpool. Following a joint investigation, we believed that they were planning an armed attack on a bank in the Allerton area. We made this investigation our priority and eventually we discovered the date the gang would be travelling up. They were shadowed all the way by Flying Squad officers and we joined up with them as they neared our area. The robbers were observed booking into a sumptuous hotel in the city centre.

From the moment they entered the hotel we kept it under 24-hour surveillance. Throughout the evening and the night they did not stir from the premises but were seen drinking in the bar. The following morning, just after dawn, I was back on observations with my team. We were aware that these were dangerous men. They were already suspected of committing armed robberies not only in London but in several provincial cities. On several of these, shots had been discharged. We had no intention of allowing them to commit a robbery and decided to arrest them as they were preparing to hit the bank. Had we let them go through with their intentions, there was real danger that innocent people might be injured.

Just after eleven o'clock in the morning they got into two cars and drove off. We were aware that one of these was stolen and bearing false plates. A game of cat-and-mouse began as we followed them through to the south of Liverpool. The gang were kept under constant surveillance and we noted that the car with the genuine number plates was parked up at Otterspool Promenade. This was obviously intended to be the vehicle they would make their eventual escape in. All five men transferred into the stolen car and drove off. Eventually they parked up in a side road near to the bank three miles away. Two of them alighted and were watched by some of the lads on foot. They were obviously checking the area out and eventually returned to report to their companions. After some discussion it seemed they were ready to go. The adrenaline was pumping through us as we waited for the action to begin.

They gathered at the boot of their car and began to remove two sports bags from the interior. As they did so, we hit them so fast they did not stand a chance. Even so, despite facing drawn guns, they still tried to run for it. They had no opportunity to get any distance and, after a violent struggle, were soon pinioned to the ground. Examination of their bags revealed sawn-off shotguns and stocking masks. The gang had certainly come well prepared for the robbery.

As will be appreciated, a certain amount of chaos takes place in such a stressful incident. The robbers were handcuffed, placed in police vehicles and taken to the nearby police station. On arrival, I suddenly became aware that we had six men in custody! One man was noticeably older than the rest and when I spoke to him it was clear from his strong Scouse accent that he was not from London.

'I only came out for a loaf at the corner shop!' he explained.

Unfortunately, in the mêlée a totally innocent passer-by had got caught up in the excitement. I realised he even had his pet dog with him which had followed us and was now yelping outside the station door! He was quickly released with the most fulsome apologies but he did not turn a hair. He told me that we had a hard job to do and happily went on his way to complete his errand. I shudder to think what would happen these days about such an error in this far more litigious climate.

The five remaining men were handed over to the Flying Squad officers to be returned to London and dealt with for their crimes. All in all, it was a superb result.

Chapter Twenty-Nine

The Somali club was a well-frequented popular night rendezvous at the top of Parliament Street. In the early hours of one Saturday morning 28-year-old Kenneth was found with serious chest injuries at the bottom of the stairs leading to the toilets. He was rushed to hospital but died shortly afterwards from a knife wound to the heart – he had been killed on a night out to celebrate his birthday. Most of the people in the club had been taken to St Annes Street station where I arrived just before dawn. I was delighted to be working with Detective Chief Inspector John Ralphson in what turned out to be his last murder inquiry before he retired. John had been my detective sergeant in the Commando Squad and had given me the confidence that I had the makings of a detective.

I had conducted a number of interviews with patrons who had been present at the club and I was bringing John up to date when the telephone rang. By now the news of the murder had been broadcast on the local radio and in the press. John answered the telephone and, when he replaced the receiver, he looked thoughtful.

'That was the desk sergeant at Hope Street. Some

feller's walked in saying he was at the club. Come on, let's go and have a word.'

We drove across the city centre and, on entering the station, we saw a young man in his early twenties with his wife. You only had to look at their faces. The hunt was over.

And so it was. He fully admitted becoming involved in a stupid, drunken argument which had led to the pointless death of a young man, leaving a widow and two orphaned young children. He told us that he had dumped the knife that he had used in the slaying down a grid in nearby St Saviour's Square. A thorough search did not result in the weapon being found. He then volunteered to draw a sketch of the weapon, using a pen supplied by his solicitor. This confirmed to some extent that it was the type of knife used in the stabbing. In due course, he was sentenced to life imprisonment.

A few days later I was giving Mike a lift back from court to Admiral Street. As I was driving along Princess Avenue, passing the Rialto, a Ford Cortina ahead of us with three men aboard suddenly accelerated away. It was obvious they had recognised that we were in an unmarked police car and a high-speed pursuit commenced through the back streets. As we careered around a corner the back-seat passenger hurled open his door and flung himself from the fast-moving vehicle. Cursing, I had to swerve to avoid him as he bounced along the roadway and I continued the chase. To my total disbelief at the next corner the front-seat passenger repeated this manic behaviour! How he didn't fall under the wheels of an oncoming lorry I will never know.

Shortly after this, the driver of the car lost it on a

bend. The vehicle skewed across the road and came to a sudden halt, the front of the car crumpled against a house wall. Mike and I ran over and found the driver unharmed, if a little shaken up. We then were somewhat perturbed to discover that the vehicle was his own.

'What's the score, pal? Why the hell did your mates risk getting killed?'

'Dunno.'

'This is your car, right?'

'Yeah.'

Mike did a radio check and discovered that there was a warrant in existence for the driver, who had failed to answer his bail at the Crown Court for burglary. He was arrested but refused to tell us who his passengers had been.

A few days later, Tom rang me regarding this incident. A contact had informed him that these men were on their way to do a robbery and had panicked on seeing us. There was little we could do other than log them for future attention. As Tom pointed out, it may have been just as well that we had not stopped them in the car under the circumstances. They had certainly been desperate enough to avoid arrest, so how would they have reacted in a confrontation if they were armed? It brought back memories of the mid-sixties when I was one of hundreds of officers who had attended a remembrance service at Liverpool cathedral dedicated to three Metropolitan police officers. Christopher Head. Geoffrey Fox and David Wombwell had been gunned down by the occupants of a car they had stopped in similar circumstances. Out on the streets, such a thought was always at the back of your mind.

*

The vicinity of Aigburth Road is a very respectable residential area. One of the larger homes had been bought by a society helping the homeless and was used as a halfway house. The residents stayed there until they were settled into a permanent address as and when vacancies arose. I had dealings with them and had built up a good rapport. Many of the occupants had fallen on hard times through no fault of their own and some of their stories made you count your blessings. I had been able to help out on occasions with a variety of problems but unfortunately not all of my colleagues displayed the same compassion or understanding.

I received an urgent call to go there one morning and, as I got out of my car, I was met by Mary, one of the long-term residents, and Roy, the manager. I was a little bewildered by the tale that unfolded. In the early hours of the morning, three masked men had gained entry, one armed with a pistol, the other two with hammers, and had threatened the residents. They gagged and tied them up and ransacked the flats. Finding nothing of real value, they had taken Roy out of the flats and beaten him up to make him reveal where anything else was hidden. He had then been dumped back at the house. After about an hour, he had managed to free himself and raise the alarm. Now, this was a nasty intimidating crime but it had one extremely puzzling feature. It was obviously a well-planned job and the offenders had come armed, but for what? Hardly anyone there had two pennies to rub together so what had they hoped to achieve? The police from Garston had attended and taken details of the offence but, frankly, Mary had not been very impressed by what she had felt was their disinterested attitude. In view of this she held back one piece of vital information. She had recognised one of the gang – knew him very well in fact. Eric Little had been the boyfriend for several months of a young single mother who had stayed there.

'Why didn't you tell them, Mary?'

'They talked down to us, Mr Mulloy. We know you'll do something about it!'

One of the things that had been drummed into me as a young detective by Tom Hall was how important it was to deal with people. Even if you did not have a snowball's chance in hell of clearing a job up, you always gave the impression that no stone would be left unturned in your endeavours. In Tom's eyes not only did the public need to have that confidence in you, but it cost you nothing and who could say what they may ring you about in the future? It had paid off for me many, many times.

The total value of the haul, if you could call it that, was only a few quid and normally I would have just passed the information on to the division. Not because of the low value, I must stress, but it would have been the normal procedure to follow. However, on this occasion, I decided to investigate the lead myself.

Fortunately, both Tom and Mike were in the division and we liaised in the inquiry. Eric Little, the man we wanted, was a small-time thief in his late twenties with a string of petty convictions and this type of job seemed out of his league. The other two men had been heard to have London accents and they had seemed to be annoyed with him when they were looking for valuables. We soon discovered that Little had been out of town for some months, living somewhere in the Tottenham Court Road area of London. Eventually Tom and Mike got an address for him and he was nicked down there on our request.

We travelled down by inter-city train to interview Little. He threw his hands up to the job right away and named the other two men concerned. He was most earnest in one request though.

'Look, lads, they're already pissed off with me. Don't say I gave them up.'

'Yeah, I heard they seemed annoyed with you. What was that about?'

'It cost them more to do the job than we got out of it!'

We arrested the other two suspects and eventually the whole story unfolded. Little had been on the run, wanted for failing to appear at court for theft. He'd headed for London, got himself a flat and started to drink in the local dives. He put it about that he was a desperate man on the run from Liverpool and pretended to be an armed robber to impress his listeners. He invented many fictitious blags he had carried out and boasted of the next job he was planning – to rob a house in Aigburth stuffed with antiques worth countless thousands of pounds. Now, he knew that the only antiques there were the cooking pots but it must have impressed the other two guys. They made enquiries with contacts of their own in Liverpool and were correctly told this was a good-class area, so his story sounded right.

Little was told by his new friends that they would do the job with him and he was now in a quandary. He was afraid to lose face so he carried on as if his information was correct! Obviously, the charade ended when they actually did the job. Not only had they run a high risk carrying a gun, it cost them more to hire the car they travelled up in than the profit they made from their meagre haul! Neither were they too impressed by the heavy prison sentences they eventually got for robbery and kidnapping.

On his eventual release, Little must have returned to London. The last I heard of him was when Mike and I were talking to Linda, a pretty dark-haired barmaid in the Metal Box club in Speke.

'You arrested Eric Little a few times, didn't you?'

'Yes we did why. Why Linda?'

'Just been sent down in the Smoke, hasn't he?'

'What for?'

'Stabbed a copper, so I heard.'

At last he had the notoriety he so desperately wanted.

Chapter Thirty

'Where is she, Mike?' Gordon McKenzie asked me as he walked into the flat in New Henderson Street, Toxteth early one Saturday morning.

'Through here, sir,' I replied.

He followed me into the tiny bedroom and we both looked at the crumpled, fragile body on the bed. For all the world she was everyone's idea of what a gentle grey-haired granny should look like. Susannah was a crippled 84-year-old spinster who had been found asphyxiated in her home a short while earlier. Together we examined the body and then made a brief examination of the room.

'Why is it always you on a Saturday?' he asked me.

Well, he may have been the boss, but Carol certainly had a more forceful way of asking the same question! I must admit that I either landed a job on a weekend or got called out to one.

'What have we go so far?'

'Not a lot, Mr Mac. Her handbag is here with over £12 inside. It seems to be her pension money. The electric meter's been broken into and the window of the kitchen may have been forced. I've checked with the division – there were the usual number of break-ins overnight. One of interest is another old lady's flat. Screwed the same way last night over in Beaufort Street and a few quid stolen. Oh yes, I've just been told on the radio there's an old dear at the nick saying she may be able to help. I've called everyone out, that's it so far sir.'

'OK. You go and see what the old girl wants and set up the Murder Control. I'll see you later.'

I booked myself out with the uniformed officer who was keeping an attendance log, thankful that at least it looked like I would miss the required post-mortem examination. In an interview room I spoke to the elderly lady who had called in. She was anxious to help in any way, having heard the news of the tragedy on local radio. She told me that she had trouble sleeping because of the racket made by late-night revellers passing her ground-floor flat. Somewhere after midnight she had been lying awake when she heard three ear-splitting screams. They were so blood-curdling she had got out of bed but had seen nothing on the street. She had been so upset she had been unable to sleep all night. As I listened to this chilling account from a distressed old woman I realised she had probably heard the last sounds the deceased had made on earth.

I told Gordon of this latest development and began to set up the control room. The murder bags were brought over from our office. We had no computers in those days but these cases contained just about everything we needed, from pens to every conceivable form to be filled in. Being so experienced, the officers from the squad who were to perform the administrative roles needed little guidance.

It was generally felt that Susannah's murder was a

case of a petty burglary gone wrong, the offender being disturbed and panicking. The following Monday I was due at an armed robbery trial at the Crown Court so I played no further part in the investigations but, a few nights later in the bar at HQ, Gordon told me that this was indeed what it had turned out to be. The man responsible was arrested very shortly after the inquiry began, being taken into custody following inquiries into the activities of local burglars. And the price of the life of an innocent old lady who had never harmed anyone? Less than fifty pence – which was the grand amount stolen from her meter.

Susannah had had her life snuffed out for less than the cost of a packet of cigarettes. What sense did all this make?

What started off as a favour ended up as a record in Liverpool for the number of persons appearing on indictment at the Crown Court. On average my section alone would be looking into several armed robberies somewhere in the city. We were running at a detection rate of over 70 per cent, but having to deal with very dangerous men while carrying firearms was becoming to be a strain on all of us.

At one time things were reasonably quiet. Detective Sergeant Neil Mcateer and Ray Murray were two hard-working lads, always looking for action. They approached me one day about a case they wanted to look into. Neil knew a retired policeman who was the chief security officer for a large foodstuffs manufacturer. This man was looking into a series of high-value thefts from their main depot. Though the stock kept disappearing, he was getting nowhere and was now asking for our help. Having talked it over with him, we decided to take it on board. Within a couple of weeks we had nicked one driver who rolled over, and what he told us opened everything up. He was just a cog in an intricate conspiracy that started at the very top. The depot had only been open for a year but, practically from day one, stock had been haemorrhaging by the pallet-load. On many occasions, whole lorry loads had been filched and sold on.

What had seemed to be a quick in-and-out inquiry eventually rolled on for over six months. We travelled all over the North West searching shops and premises and recovering hundreds of thousands of pounds worth of gear. To give an idea of how much we were seizing, the firm had to rent warehouses in the Widnes area for the recovered goods to be stored. Our property system would not have been able to cope with the demand. On top of that, they had two men and a pantechnicon on permanent standby to rendezvous with us as and when required to transport the property we were recovering.

Even we were surprised how complex the conspiracy was. We were hitting premises who had no contract for their goods and discovering that practically the entire stock was stolen.

Several premises had even had extensions built to house the goods they had not yet sold! One man we took out was known as the 'Squire' he was so wealthy but how much he had amassed as a result of this fiddle was difficult to assess. He received five years for his part in the enterprise.

Eventually we nabbed fourteen of the firm's staff, nine shopkeepers, a supermarket owner and ten others who had helped in the distribution. Judge Lawton was scathing in his comments.

'I have to take such a course which makes it clear to others that such a swindle will not be tolerated.' He sentenced them to lengthy terms of imprisonment.

Chapter Thirty-One

When I was running the Robbery Squad a couple of years earlier, we arrested a man for what the trial judge described as 'the most reckless and callous piece of driving I have ever heard of'. A stolen car was being pursued by a mobile patrol unit in Upper Warwick Street, Toxteth, and a very young constable stepped into the road and waved at the driver to stop. It was a brave but foolhardy action. He was mown down and received serious injuries, including a triple fracture of the pelvic bone.

The driver escaped but we received information as to his identity. Three weeks later we raided a flat at dawn in nearby Berkeley Walk and nicked him. When we arrested him he was no hero, shaking with fear and apprehensive that we may take retribution. In this he was to be disappointed, he was dealt with like any other prisoner and was later sent to prison. Little did I know that I was subsequently to have dealings with him in probably one of the most appalling matters that I have ever encountered.

Little Darryn was a three-year-old doted on by all his relatives. In his short life he was described as having brought only joy and happiness to those who knew him.

His 24-year-old mother came from a large, close-knit family. The only cloud on the horizon was that since the age of sixteen she had associated on and off with the man who had knocked down the constable. He was also twenty-four years of age but was not the father of her child.

She lived in a flat not far from her family and was constantly in touch with her relatives, all of whom said she adored her child. In the weeks leading up to Christmas 1977, her family noticed a change in her and also in Darryn. He seemed to be withdrawn, when usually he was a boisterous little lad. It was noticed on occasions he had suffered bruising. The bruises were explained away by his mother but still a nagging doubt remained with her family. When they actually challenged her with their suspicions that her boyfriend was responsible for these injuries she emphatically denied it.

Real concern arose on Christmas Day. All the family gathered at the parents' home but neither Darryn, whose presents lay under the Christmas tree, nor his mother arrived, although they were due for dinner. The family's fears increased when they discovered that the mother was no longer living where they thought she was. The family made their own enquiries, not knowing by now she was staying with the man they did not approve of.

On Boxing Day, having made a fruitless search, family members called at Admiral Street Police Station, poignantly carrying Darryn's gifts. They reported their worries regarding the child. They told the desk officer that his mother had recently taken the boy to Alder Hey

Hospital with bruising to his face. The police checked there but there was no record of him being treated. Now the alarm bells in the family's minds began ringing, loud and insistent.

The police spent the day trying to trace the child. Unfortunately, because of his nomadic life style, the boyfriend had a number of addresses but he was not found at any of them. The matter was then passed on to the Social Services Department, as is the routine procedure.

At 8 p.m. on Monday, 16th January, screaming hysterically, Darryn's mother battered on a neighbour's door. She cried she could not wake Darryn and the neighbour urgently summoned an ambulance. Darryn was brought downstairs by his mother. He was shaking uncontrollably, his eyes were staring vacantly, two of his bottom teeth were missing and he was dribbling blood from his mouth. The common-law husband stayed upstairs and made no effort to accompany them.

Darryn was rushed to the Liverpool Children's Hospital and was immediately placed on a life-support system. He was suffering from a dreadful catalogue of injuries. The doctors were horror-struck by his condition and the nurses, even though used to suffering and the sight of severe injury, wept with compassion for the little mite.

We were called in to assist the division and would have normally been met with friendly, ribald comments. Not this time. Everyone, and I mean everyone, was affected as the case began to unfold. In the future there would be criticism of the police and social services for the alleged breakdown in communication in this case. That would come with hindsight.

The boy's mother and her common-law husband were taken into custody and questioned about his condition. It seemed that the attention his mother gave him was resented by her boyfriend. A picture emerged that showed that little Darryn had been the victim of what can only described as a sustained bout of torture by the man. He had been so terrified he had soiled his bed and this had kept alive the vicious circle of beatings. The final attack came when the small tot spilt tea on the carpet. This childish accident cost him his life. A neighbour spoke of hearing him being beaten for ten minutes, so much so that it made her feel ill. The last days of his existence were spent in agony.

Darryn never recovered consciousness and on Saturday, 21st January, his life-support system was switched off. The toddler had lost his battle for life, having lain still and silent since his admission. The nurses who had fought day and night as he clung to existence were shattered. Although we had been expecting it, a pall of gloom descended on the inquiry team.

At a hushed Crown Court some months later, the common-law husband pleaded guilty to the manslaughter of the child. Counsel for the Crown claimed that Darryn had had scalding liquid poured over his legs and burns to his foot. These injuries had been sustained over some days and had left him in excruciating pain. Most sickeningly, part of his penis had been cut off with a pair of nail clippers. When the final attack came, Darryn had been too weak to resist any longer.

After spilling the tea on the carpet he had been struck

and then shaken so violently he had become unconscious. The 'man' responsible for this sat with his head bowed in the dock as counsel told the court that throughout his agonising ordeal little Darryn put on an incredibly brave face. 'He would not cry, even when I hit him,' his assailant had told the police officers in interview.

A sad epitaph for such a short life.

The common-law husband eventually received fifteen years' imprisonment for manslaughter. He was wise enough to immediately request that he be isolated from other inmates. He would have known what to expected. Darryn's mother went down for eighteen months for wilfully neglecting her son.

No officer who worked on that inquiry was untouched. Inevitably, when the case was publicised there was an outcry. Did Darryn have to die in such tragic circumstances? was the question being asked. I have no answer.

Chapter Thirty-Two

A man was wanted for wounding his ex-girlfriend. Unable to accept her rejection, he had turned up drunk at her Croxteth home in the early hours of the morning and smashed his way inside. Following a violent argument, he had savagely beaten her. We already knew him as a city centre doorman with a penchant for violence. Don Jones and I had learnt that he had arranged to meet someone in the Brookhouse pub, just near the bottom of Smithdown Road on the fringes of Murder Mile. Our informant also added that he was nearly always carrying a shooter, either on him or in his car. For a nice change we had time to put together a plan, rather than having to take hasty action.

Just after 7 p.m. on a lovely summer's night, I sat with my lads in a squad car on the garage forecourt opposite the pub. We saw him drive up in his vehicle and enter the pub. I already had some squad men inside waiting to observe him and warn us on the radio when he was leaving. Several other cars were scattered about the area, including two marked police cars which contained the Firearms Unit in full uniform. We had reason to believe this was one mad man who would resist arrest by any means. Our thinking was to allow him to leave the

237

pub and follow him until he came to a halt in traffic. The marked units, backed up by us, would then swoop. For over an hour we waited in the stifling car with the tension rising until the call came.

We watched our target reverse his car and then drive out along Smithdown Road in the direction of the city. We were two vehicles behind him and, as he approached the lights at Gainsborough Road, they changed against our traffic flow. We had him bottled in the traffic queue and urgently passed the message. Within seconds, with a wail of klaxons, two marked cars raced up, the doors were flung open and he was caught cold. He was ringed by high-velocity weapons pointing at him and he was ordered in no uncertain terms to leave the car, keep his hands in view and lie face down on the roadway.

He had been taken absolutely by surprise and certainly was in no position to argue. Slowly he clambered out, looked at the menace that faced him and complied. As he lay face down an officer pinioned his arms with plastic handcuffs behind his back. Now these actions obviously drew quite a lot of interest from other motorists and passers-by. Astoundingly, one old woman completely misunderstood what was going on. Striding through the onlookers, she looked down at our prisoner before giving him words of advice.

'Serves you right, you bastard. It's about time the police did something about bloody speeders like you, racing down the road!'

John Gaffney turned to me with a grin as we holstered our guns. We were all coming down from a high of adrenaline and she was just the tonic we needed.

'Bloody hell, boss, I wonder how she would like us to deal with burglars?'

My section was balancing not only our own inquiries but was stretched to the limit on many other cases. We had completed two separate rape inquiries over attacks on young girls, both on the Wirral. Just after 5 o'clock on a Saturday afternoon, a twelve-year-old girl was making her way home after buying some sweets. She cut through the underpass in New Ferry and she was followed by a man. He attacked her and dragged her into the nearby New Ferry Park where she was forced to strip off her clothes and was subjected to a savage sexual attack. The initial assault occurred in a residential area and the public were of great help. A 21-year-old local man was eventually arrested.

The other rape victim was even younger. Nine years of age, she was attacked in the New Brighton area in broad daylight in the Tower playgrounds. Despite many people being in the vicinity her assailant had dragged her into an entry under the racetrack and sexually abused her. Inquiries resulted in a male being charged with the attack.

We were tied up in several robbery inquiries when another – which had not even been committed in this country – was added to the pile. For some years Joyce had been my informant and, although I could not describe her as prolific, she was always very accurate. She made contact with me and I travelled over to the Wirral to see her with John Hodson. It was worth the journey. She told us that she had heard of a serious robbery that had been carried out recently in Dublin. From what she had been told some men had attacked a jeweller's shop in the city and taken practically the entire stock. Although she had absolutely no idea who had committed the offence, she knew that the stolen property was being offered for sale in Liverpool. Hugh, the man who was attempting to sell it, was very cagey but she reckoned she could arrange a meet with him if he thought that she would bring along a prospective buyer.

Joyce only knew Hugh by his first name but was familiar with the system he used as he was a prolific handler of stolen goods. Any prospective buyer had to contact him by telephoning a public house in the Princess Drive area of Liverpool and asking for him by an assumed name. Although wary, he was anxious to dispose of the property as soon as possible. I asked Joyce if her involvement would place her in any danger and she assured me it wouldn't. She worked in various massage parlours but Hugh had no idea of her address or what her real name was.

'Let's be honest, Mr Mulloy, they're not interested in your face when you're doin' the business with them, are they?' she said.

We returned to the office and John began telephone inquiries to Dublin. Within a short time he had confirmed that such an offence had occurred two days earlier. Everything Joyce had told us appeared to be accurate. What was surprising was how quickly the gear had arrived in Liverpool and been put on offer. We called back to see Joyce and, in our presence, she rang Hugh at the pub and made arrangements to meet him at noon the next day.

At eleven o'clock the following morning we were in place in the pub car park, concealed in the rear of a covert observation van. It was just as well that we were, as this man turned out to be a very cautious creature. Shortly afterwards, a Cortina entered the car park and drove slowly around, checking parked vehicles before exiting. Joyce positively identified the driver as our target. She was then swiftly driven away by a member of our team while we awaited developments. Twice more the Cortina repeated this manoeuvre until, finally, some twenty minutes after the appointed time, he parked up and entered the pub.

After half an hour he returned to the car and, as he was about to unlock the door, we approached him. The boot was unlocked and, in a large sports bag, we found thirteen plastic shopping bags. When these were opened they contained a number of rings, charms, watches and bracelets. As a result of what he later told us in interview, two more search warrants were executed in homes at Maghull and Whiston and a further large quantity of jewellery was recovered. Two days later we met a coaster ship that made regular trips between Dublin and England, and arrested the crew member who was acting as the courier.

Within hours of the robbery the goods had been steaming out of Dublin. It appeared that we had recovered the stock of the shop almost in its entirety. The owner was ecstatic as he had facing going out of business. Now he was desperate to have his property back so that he could continue trading. We made arrangements for him to fly into Liverpool and met him at the airport. He identified the property as his and confirmed that we had recovered nearly all of it. He was one very happy man. All those we arrested later went to prison for handling stolen goods.

On another occasion, a petty argument between two criminals nearly ended in death. Eddie, a man of violence with numerous convictions, was greatly feared by many people. One lunchtime he was sitting in a pub in Kirkby on the outskirts of the city when Harry, man he had previously threatened, entered and approached him. Customers and staff scattered in all directions as Harry pulled out a handgun and pointed it directly at Eddie, who sat there, frozen with fear. Harry pulled the trigger and fired several shots but even at that short range he missed! Then Harry fled from the pub.

A few days later, Tom and I entered the Hanover Hotel in the city centre late one evening. We were chatting and, as Tom was ordering our drinks, I glanced around the crowded bar. I quickly turned back.

'Tom, over by the door. Isn't that Harry who's wanted for that shooting job the other day?'

Tom studied the room through the bar mirror and confirmed that I was right.

'Who's that he's with, Mike?'

'It's years since I've seen her but I'm sure that's his wife.'

'If it's his missus he won't want any bother.'

'He's nearly finished his drink. If we try and get to the phone he'll see us.'

'Hang on just a minute.'

Tom attracted the attention of the barmaid and ordered two scotches. We downed them in one gulp and looked at one another.

'Let's take him.'

We approached the table and stood looking down on him, alert for any sudden movement. He looked up and, on recognising us, became resigned to his fate.

'Evenin' Mr Hall, Mr Mulloy. No trouble, lads, just let's say goodbye to the wife.'

True to his word, he surrendered meekly enough. In fairness, when he had committed this latest crime he had stepped well out of his league. We took him to the Main Bridewell and booked him in. The divisional lads dealing with the incident would collect him from there and I thought little more about it.

Some months later I was at court when I met one of the sergeants who had dealt with the case. We sat together in the canteen and he reminded me of the arrest.

'How did he get on?' I asked.

'Got four years, pleaded guilty.'

'Four years, I suppose that's about right.'

'Not really. I reckon the judge would have given him probation if he had shot that fat bastard Eddie. He got sent down for missing!'

Chapter Thirty-Three

One Sunday morning I walked into Upton Police Station, which was not far from my home. I was supposed to be on a rest day but I was leading my section looking into an armed robbery at the nearby dairy that had happened the Friday before. Three masked raiders, two armed with shotguns, had taken the cash office out and escaped with five thousand pounds. We eventually nicked the lads who had done it but events that morning were to overtake me.

I was having a coffee with Kevin Cronin when I was called to the telephone. It was an inspector from the division at Birkenhead who told me that a girl had been attacked during the night and he asked for our assistance. We drove the few miles there and he outlined what had happened.

Just after three in the morning an eighteen-year-old girl had been discovered, naked and unconscious, in the North End area of Birkenhead. Her clothing had been found ripped from her body and strewn about the alley in which she lay. She had been viciously raped and battered about the head and body. Kevin and I went to Birkenhead General Hospital and I was appalled at the sight of her injuries. The medical staff would not commit themselves on her chances of survival as she was suffering from a fractured skull. For three days she lay in intensive care before regaining consciousness. The attacker had to be caught or the next victim could well be killed.

The girl was a popular local lass and part of a close family, well known and liked in the vicinity. She had been at a wedding reception in a nearby house that night and had offered to return home to collect some records. As she had made her way back she had become the victim of a thug with a sick mind. The whole local community, especially her family, were distraught by the severity of the assault. Her parents could not even recognise her so bad were her facial injuries. They were utterly bewildered that this could happen to their daughter. The locals rallied around, sending countless cards and gifts to the hospital and offering any support to the family that they may need. Just as important, they came forward to assist the inquiry with information.

George Penny, who was now posted to the division, worked with us and we looked at another similar attack. Both girls were alike in appearance and both offences had occurred near to each other. The second victim was also eighteen years old and, as she had walked down a side road, she had been dragged into an entry. Her throat had been gripped so tightly she could hardly breathe and couldn't scream. Her attacker threatened to kill her if she made a sound and told her she would be stabbed if she did not remove her clothing. She was then flung to the floor and savagely raped.

The hunt continued and one night, several days into the inquiry, I finished going over the last batch of statements in the deserted office and looked at my watch. To my surprise it was after 1 a.m. Stretching, I yawned and gathered my coat, ready for my home and bed. As I was about to leave the station, a young female reporter from the local radio station came through the front door. She requested a brief interview about the crime and, although tired, I agreed as I knew the value of publicity. It was a fairly standard interview, I repeated what had occurred and made a request for any witnesses to come forward. In passing, I mentioned that some people may have thought the assault was the result of a dispute between a couple. This would not have been unusual, bearing in mind the area and time of the incident. People may not have realised that an innocent girl was being attacked. Having finished the interview, I thought no more of it.

The following morning I was having breakfast in the canteen at the nick when a local superintendent joined our table.

'I heard your interview on the seven o'clock news, Michael. Very professional, I would say, apart from one thing.'

'What was that?'

'You said words to the effect that a man and a woman rowing in the street in that area is not unusual. Local residents may not like it.'

The table fell silent and everyone looked at him. Did this fellow ever go out or leave his office? Was he aware of how stretched his officers could get on the first couple of hours on a night shift in that patch? Biting my tongue on such comments, I sarcastically made a suggestion.

'Sorry if you did not agree with what I said about your area. Tell you what, in future I will contact you to do the interviews if you wish.'

'Yes,' he replied somewhat frostily, 'that may make for a better balance.'

A couple of days passed and once again I was leaving the nick when I met the same reporter. She was there about a different matter, but there was no way I was going to pass this up. It was just before two in the morning, probably about the worst time to be woken up.

'Good morning, sir, DI Mulloy, here. We have a radio reporter asking for an interview. Should I put her on?'

A moment's silence passed, then the dialling tone came over the line as the receiver was slammed down. I saw him many times in the years to come but he never mentioned this incident to me once. Mind you, thinking about it, he rarely spoke to me at all after that.

Eventually, following information from the public, we arrested a man in connection with these attacks. He was an arrogant villain and full of himself. He pleaded guilty at the Crown Court to one of the attacks and was told by the judge: 'This rape is as callous a crime as I've ever came across.'

He was sentenced to six years' imprisonment with a further year for an unprovoked attack on a man he had never seen before in his life.

Over the years I've been fortunate to have been commended on a number of occasions. In reality these commendations are merely pieces of paper which are now gathering dust in my attic. Of far more importance to me have been the spontaneous letters of appreciation I have received from innocent victims or their families. I was very touched to receive such a missive from the mother of the young girl in this case, thanking me for the attention and assistance given to her and her family. She wrote that she found herself unable to put into words how much my hard work had made her family happy. When I called to thank her, she hugged me and said I had helped all the family come through the nightmare. Now that is what I call a commendation from the heart.

Chapter Thirty-Four

We seemed to be spending a lot of our time on the Wirral and were now engaged with two serious robberies. For a change, these were not wages blags but attacks on private homes. Both occurred over the same weekend and were despicable, cowardly crimes.

The first took place late on a Friday night when four stocking-masked men, one dressed as a police officer, called at a house in St Margaret's Road in Hoylake. They forced their way into the dwelling and threatened to shoot the householder and his wife with a sawn-off shotgun. Beating them about the head, they forced the man to open his safe and stole jewellery with a value of over £23,000.

As a part of this inquiry we looked at similar offences in the north-west of England. There had been a number where a bogus policeman in uniform had been used to gain admittance. The terror and violence these men were prepared to use was frightening. One victim had been threatened with castration and having his teenage daughter raped. Another man had his testicles bitten to force him to reveal a safe combination. Severe beatings were commonplace. In yet another, a woman was tied up along with her young Down's syndrome daughter and her son, who was also threatened with castration.

Although there was no direct connection, when we eventually arrested those suspected for the Hoylake robbery we were surprised to find a Cockney among them. He was a violent, cruel man who was shattered by his arrest. He had been well prepared to give it out when the odds were stacked in his favour, but when we took him out he was certainly no hero. He was well off his area and decided to become a 'supergrass', not for us but for the Metropolitan Police. This was a system in vogue at the time. Such men would admit serious offences, implicating their friends and being prepared to give evidence against them, not out of remorse but merely to obtain a lighter sentence. The Cockney had obviously made his own approaches to the Met and, completely without our knowledge, they had him transferred back down south.

He was being dealt with by the robbery section of the Flying Squad and I travelled down with Frank Carthy to interview him again, regarding other matters. He was being held at a purposely converted high-security police station with others of his ilk. He was not too happy to see us, not that we cared. I was quite content to see that his memories of Liverpool were not good ones. He was part of a gang who were prepared to use threats and extreme violence and this evil thug was certainly getting no favours from us. It made my skin crawl just to be in the same room as him. I made no attempt to hide my distaste and to ensure that he was fully aware that, no matter what favours he may expect from his new-found 'friends', he could expect none from me.

On their eventual appearance at the Crown Court

the judge told the robbers: 'You were members of an armed gang recruited to carry out the most terrible robberies which have caused havoc throughout the country.'

Well-deserved sentences of up to fifteen years were handed down.

The other robbery occurred on a Sunday morning. Westwood Road is a quiet tree-lined avenue of palatial homes near to the centre of Upton village, about three miles from Birkenhead town centre. One such house, set in its own grounds was owned by a millionaire property-developer. At the time of this offence, his wife, his thirty-year-old daughter and her nine-month-old baby daughter were also in residence. After the family had breakfasted, the husband left for his round of golf at the local course – his usual Sunday morning activity. Something was about to occur that was far removed from custom and his wife and daughter were to suffer a terrifying experience. Shortly after he had gone, his wife was busying herself making the beds and his daughter was in the rear of the house. Both women were still in their nightwear, it was a beautiful morning and the baby lay in her pram just outside the front door, taking advantage of the sunshine. This door was slightly ajar so her mother could hear if she cried.

A car was heard in the driveway and three masked men burst into the house. The mother was grabbed, menaced with a hammer and thrown onto a bed. Despite being an elderly lady, she was lashed to a central-heating radiator. The gang demanded the combination of the safe and threatened to batter her to death with the hammer if she did not comply. She became very confused so they dragged her into the bedroom where the safe was and threatened her with a gun. She was repeatedly told they would beat her face in, while she pleaded with them not to touch her daughter or grandchild.

Her daughter, having heard her mother scream, had come running out of her room when she was grabbed by another masked male and threatened with a crowbar. She was pulled into the kitchen and made to lie on the floor. She could hear her mother screaming and the thug told her that she and her mother would be killed if they did not keep quiet. As she lay in her nightwear she told her guard that she was pregnant. This was a white lie. In her terror-stricken state of mind, dressed as she was, she feared being sexually attacked. It is hard to imagine the dread both of them were in.

After repeated pleadings, the two women and the baby were put together in the main bedroom. By this time the older woman was hysterical, having been repeatedly told she was going to be shot if she did not reveal the combination to the safe. She was in such a panic she could not recall the numbers. In exasperation, one of the gang hurled a heavy cigarette-lighter into the carry-cot which contained the baby. Fortunately his aim was not accurate.

Eventually the gang ripped the safe from the wall with chisels and escaped with several thousands of pounds worth of cash and jewellery. They abandoned the women who were still locked in the bedroom. These women suffered extreme terror at the hands of these thugs. We were later to discover that one of the gang was quite prepared to drop the baby onto her head to force the combination from her grandmother. Many months later they still suffered from the mental agony, unable to stay in the house alone or venture out at night, even by car.

Having been called in, my section took control of the inquiry. House-to-house inquiries were carried out and we began to trawl through our informants. Within a few days we had a promising lead. We had an informant who had proved his worth to us on a number of serious crime inquiries. He made contact and I met him in the American Bar in Lime Street in the city centre. He told me that he knew two of the men responsible for this attack but only by sight. That evening he was due to meet them in the Masonic pub in Lark Lane, just down the road from the police station. They had promised to show him samples of jewellery they were eager to dispose of. That night we covered the venue both inside and out but, to our frustration, they failed to show up.

However, the next day the informant was on the telephone to me with what we needed. He told me one of the men we were seeking was Roger Wise and gave us his address in Pelham Grove, off Lark Lane. This villain was a big, burly ex-boxer who was already on bail for high-class house raids. He was a professional criminal with numerous previous convictions and a reputation as a reckless, yet competent, getaway driver. My contact was also able to give details of Wise's background and associates and we completed a prodigious amount of work within hours. It was well after midnight when I drove home, my mind full of the anticipated confrontation the following day.

Just after 7 a.m. the next day we arrived at Wise's flat.

We were again armed. My contact had warned me that the gang habitually carried firearms themselves. Aside from some threats and bluster we had little trouble and Wise was arrested and taken to Birkenhead Police Station.

The interview that took place was critical to the progress of the inquiry. Wise initially denied everything but he had been badly shaken by his arrest. Eventually he began to crack. First of all, he tried to persuade us that he had been invited to go on the robbery but had declined. Finally he threw his hand in and gave us his version of the role that he had played. He told us that two cars had been used to travel to the house and that he had been one of the drivers; he had stolen the other vehicle from Parkfield Place in Liverpool.

He alleged that he had remained in the car while four other men had entered the house. He stated that they were carrying firearms and, after committing the robbery, they had placed the safe in his car. The stolen car had been dumped off Conway Street in Birkenhead and he had driven the other members of the gang to an address in Liverpool. He told us that the raid had been planned for weeks and his eventual written statement revealed the depth of organisation that had been involved, even down to timed practice runs. He was adamant he did not know the identity of his fellow robbers other than one known to him as 'Cockney John' who was employed as a joiner at a local building firm. As our informant had also told us, he said that Cockney John nearly always carried a firearm on his person. According to him, these men were all violent and at least two were from Birmingham. Travelling outside their local area to commit crime was a popular trend at the time for professional robbers. Because Wise had admitted the offence and told us what he knew, he was now in fear for his own safety. That, coming from a violent man, showed the pedigree of this gang more than anything.

Kevin Cronin and I made inquiries at a local builders and we soon had a second name. Cockney John was, in fact, John Bellis and his firm had carried out several jobs at the property-developer's house. We then commenced observation on his home. Bellis was well steeped in crime, with many previous convictions. By chance I had got him his last one. I had searched his home when he was living in the Lark Lane district and recovered the proceeds from a shop that had been broken into. He had been convicted of receiving stolen goods.

At about 5 p.m. Bellis was seen to approach his house and we arrested him as he was about to enter the front door. His home was searched and, as this took place, he asked to speak to me. I took him into the kitchen with Kevin and he told me he remembered our previous encounter. He intimated that he was willing to do a deal for the return of the jewellery. I told him that we could sort matters out in his formal interview and, after the search was concluded, he was taken to Birkenhead Police Station.

This man was something of an enigma, even to people who had known him for years. A man of few words and even less emotion, he was difficult to interview, being constantly guarded in what he said. During the initial interview, it came out that he had in fact fitted the safe in the house some ten years earlier! Eventually he was ready to admit his part in the attack. He stressed that he was terrified of the others who had taken part in the raid and feared they would harm him or his family. His written statement, made to me after I had cautioned him, was without doubt the shortest one I have ever taken in the investigation of a serious offence. All he wanted to say was: 'I admit on last Sunday at about 11 a.m. I went in the front door of Mr Ball's house in Bidston at Birkenhead. I remember seeing a For Sale sign outside. I stole the safe. There was no violence used.'

By now we had also traced a man who had been offered the chance to buy the jewellery before it had even been stolen. Our information led us again to the Masonic pub in Lark Lane on a Saturday night in search of a Dutchman who had supposedly flown into the country to buy the property. He never appeared that night, but several days later, he was arrested at Heathrow Airport with proceeds from a good-class burglary in Liverpool and also with jewellery traced to the first robbery that had occurred in St Margaret's Road.

The following Sunday we arrested Robert Power, who was on the run. We kicked in the door of a house off Queens Drive and found him hiding in a cupboard. He had been halfway through a trial at the Crown Court for theft and assault when he either got bored or, more likely, did not like the way his case was going so he failed to turn up one morning. Although we could not connect him to any of the robberies we were investigating, he had been missing for some time so it was a good capture.

Wise and Bellis appeared before the Wirral

Magistrates' Court and were remanded in custody, despite an impassioned bail application by a local solicitor. This was his first experience of dealing with us, and, during his speech, he alleged that we had smashed up one of the houses during our search.

'They may call themselves the Serious Crime Squad,' he stated, 'but I would call them the Serious Demolition Squad!'

We were flattered by his remarks!

No more arrests were made and eventually the case came to trial at the Crown Court before Judge Patterson. John Gilchrist appeared for the Crown and the legendary late Colin Cunningam for the defence. From the outset, the onus was on attack. During the trial it was alleged by Wise that we had assaulted him when he was arrested and again during his interview. He went on to claim that he had been induced to sign his statement by fraud and, as he could not read, the contents would anyhow have been unknown to him. Bellis alleged that he had been threatened with a firearm on his arrest and that his request for a solicitor had been refused. He also alleged that his home had been severely damaged and that I had threatened to have his wife arrested unless he confessed.

I was in the witness box for three entire days, the subject of sustained and hostile cross-examination with just about every allegation being made as to my conduct. It was put to me that I had assaulted one of the defendants prior to him making his written statement. In my denials I made the following point:

'Not only did I not do that, it would have been a most inane thing to do under the circumstances.'

'Why is that?'

'I took the statement in the interview room at Birkenhead Police Station on the first floor. There are no curtains or blinds on the window so anyone could see in.'

'As it is on the first floor, who could see in?'

'It is immediately opposite the barristers' robing rooms at Birkenhead Crown Court.'

'So you allege, but that does not mean you can be seen.'

'I could have been seen. In fact, that day I saw you.'

'Where did you see me?'

'As the statement was being written I could see you getting changed in that room!'

A beautiful answer – Mr Cunningham had not seen that coming! After a hurried examination of his diary he said no more on that point. The crafty man arranged to have the view photographed later that day, though, just to be sure. On the last day of my evidence the court rose for lunch. Because I had not completed my cross-examination I had to eat alone. If I had been with my colleagues we would have been open to the accusation that I had informed them of the questions that I had been asked. Being somewhat bored, I returned to the court complex a little early. I was enjoying a last cigarette before the court was convened when one of the defence solicitors approached me.

'Well, Mr Mulloy, I must say you look a little nervous.'

OK, I accept that I borrowed it from Winston Churchill but I could not resist it.

'Yes, and you're bloody ugly. But tomorrow I will be relaxed again!'

In an effort to support their allegations of violence, the defence called Power who had gone missing during his own trial. Prior to this, Wise had told the court that had not seen Power for some four years. Power went into some detail of his arrest, during which he alleged he was assaulted by police officers. He finished his evidence and was then cross-examined by John Gilchrist.

'Did you tell the defendant Wise about this assault, prior to giving evidence in this case?'

'No.'

'Why not?'

'Just didn't.'

'But have you seen him recently?'

'Yeah, nearly every day since they got me. I see him when we exercise together in the nick.'

'Both you and he were in custody at Walton Prison, weren't you?'

'Yeah.'

'Your evidence, I take it, is that you were assaulted by officers who have given evidence in this case?'

'Yeah.'

'And your presence here is to support the allegations that these officers acted in the same way during the arrest of Wise?'

'Yeah.'

'Well, can you explain this to me? If you have never told the defendant Wise about your experiences, how do you come to be here today?'

'What?'

'You say you are here to support the evidence given in this case. How do you know what has been alleged? How would the defence possibly know what you are alleging if you have never spoken to the defendant or his solicitor about what you alleged happened to you while you were on remand together? Are you suggesting they are psychic in some way?'

There was only silence. No response at all.

'Do you suppose that his solicitors were just able to pluck you from the air and fortuitously find a corroborative witness?'

Poor Cunningham also lost out on another witness. This was a man who had been offered some stolen jewellery and had stated on oath that he only knew the defendants from a local pub and that they had never been to his home.

'Let me describe a room to you. It has a black leather suite, blue carpets, floral wallpaper, a stereo and a TV set in one corner and a large fish tank under the window. Does that mean anything to you?'

'Yeah, that sounds like my parlour.'

'How would I know that?'

'Dunno.'

'Come, come, it's obvious. I have never been to your home yet I can describe what you call your parlour. Now if I can describe that, I must have been told by one of the defendants. Yet you say you have never invited them to your home.'

'Me house got screwed last year. It must have been one of them done it!'

After a lengthy trial both men were convicted. Prior to sentence the judge addressed them: 'This is one of the most appalling cases I have encountered. These offences of robbery constitute offences of the worst kind. Both the ladies you tied up must have been terrified. You threatened them with serious physical injury and weapons. You entered masked, and those who intrude into other people's homes must lose their liberty for a considerable time. You, Bellis, helped fit the safe in that house some ten years ago. I consider you the main perpetrator of this serious offence. You knew full well what was possibly in the safe and you were quite prepared to inflict fear and terror to achieve your aims. You, Wise, I consider in a lesser role to Bellis. You never entered the home but because of your participation the offence took place. All who go to commit this type of offence must be severely punished.'

Bellis received seven years' imprisonment. Wise got four years, to be served consecutively to a term of two and a half years he was then serving for burglary, in effect a prison sentence of six and a half years.

Chapter Thirty-Five

Shortly after eight one evening I ambled into the Chidwall Five Ways pub to meet Tom and Mike for a drink. As usual, they were late so I chatted to Paula, an extremely attractive barmaid whom I had known for some years. She had lived in the Barford Road area of Hunts Cross and I had first met her when she reported the theft of some scanty underwear from her washing line. Not being the top of my priorities, it was early evening by the time I arrived at her home. In reality there was little I could do to find the pervert who had nicked her panties.

As I was leaving, she mentioned that she intended to write to the Chief Constable thanking us for our attention. I was somewhat taken aback and asked why she wished to do this. She explained that first of all a constable had come to take the report, then had called back with his sergeant. The crew of the area had popped in as they were passing, followed by the afternoon constable. Now, not only had a real-life detective called to see her, she had also had a visit from the scenes-of-crime officer!

'What did he do?' I asked incredulously.

'Oh, he was so nice. He checked the washing line for fingerprints!'

Paula had obviously been the talk of the canteen, but I talked her out of the letter. Somehow I could not see the Chief being as impressed by his 'vigilant' officers!

Coincidence often plays a part in a detective's work. I was driving around the Wirral one afternoon with Neil and eventually began to make my way back to Liverpool. As we approached the flyover in Borough Road, we received a radio message requesting that observations be kept for a hackney cab and giving part of the registration number. The passenger was wanted for a snatch from a shop in Chester city centre, some fifteen miles away. The thief had entered as a prospective purchaser and, on being shown a display of expensive rings, had grabbed the tray and fled from the shop. On the off chance, we decided to cover the Mersey Tunnel approach for half an hour. Time passed and I was considering leaving when we saw the car in question approach the toll booths. I swung my vehicle in front of it and we dived from the car and pulled open the rear door of the taxi. We grabbed the passenger and he threw his hands up right away. We recovered the jewellery and took him to Birkenhead where he was lodged to await escort from Cheshire County officers. The cab driver was an innocent party, having merely accepted a fare to Liverpool.

Information is the lifeblood of police work. I was an avid reader of all crime bulletins and, only a week or so later, I saw an entry regarding a practically identical

263

robbery that had occurred at Allerton in Liverpool. It included a sketch of the suspect and it was the same man from the Chester job! I immediately went round to his house, recovered all the gear and, once more, placed him in custody. He must have been sick of the sight of me! This time there was no bail for him.

Late one morning in Toxteth three children out playing entered a rubble strewn deadend entry. What they saw caused them to run home to their parents who, after a quick look to ascertain that the kids had not imagined things, hurriedly called the police. Lying on her back at the top of the alley was the body of 27-year-old woman, She had been strangled and had obviously been dead for many hours. Her corpse lay on an old mattress and there had been no attempt to conceal it. My section was called out to assist and, having forced our way through the heavy city centre traffic, I arrived at the scene. Divisional officers were already present and, when I examined the body, I recognised Maureen, a prostitute whom I knew slightly from the local clubs and pubs. The Murder Control was established at nearby Admiral Street and I was placed in charge of the General Enquiry Section.

Later that evening with Mike, I entered the Windsor public house where Maureen had been a regular. I spoke to many of the locals and rapidly established that she had left the bar the previous evening in the company of a male. Although we could not find anybody who knew his name we were reasonably happy. If he was a regular visitor to the area we should eventually be able to establish his identify.

Mike and I spoke to a lot of the girls, who were only too ready to help. At the back of all their minds must have been the stark thought that it could have been any one of them. Several told us that Maureen had placed the mattress in the entry herself to provide some modicum of comfort when she was performing with her clients. I found that very poignant and made me even more aware of the dreadful life style the girls were prepared to endure just to make a living.

The squad worked long hours in the determination to solve the case. It made absolutely no difference to me how she had earned her living. She was a human being whose life had been wrenched away. As can often happen, the inquiry was resolved in an unexpected manner. The murder had received extensive local publicity and some days into the inquiry a man walked into a police station and stated that he had been in Maureen's company that night. He was similar in description to the male who had left the public house with her. He was detained and interviewed by detectives on the investigation team. He eventually admitted that following a row with her he had killed her. In many ways this was a depressing case, Maureen had suffered a violent death in a dismal place after a life far too short.

A Securicor vehicle was delivering wages to a building site in the city area on Friday afternoon when the courier was attacked by three armed and masked men. After using far more violence than was necessary, they fled with the cash box containing many thousands of pounds. I arrived with Don Jones and, as we were making initial enquiries, a crowd of workers watched our every move. It was obvious that their sympathies lay with the robbers. All that dramatically changed, however, when they were informed by the foreman that they would be getting no pay until the following Monday! Having checked with our contacts, within days we were in possession of the names of the attackers. The following morning just after dawn, three armed squad teams made their way to effect the arrests. I led my section to an address in the Edge Hill district to pick up Bobby Shearer. Some years earlier I had arrested him for an armed robbery in the Allerton district. After an acrimonious trial in which the allegations flew thick and fast, he had been convicted and sent to prison for five years. Now I was looking forward to making his acquaintance again.

We smashed our way into his house and arrested him as he still lay in bed. He was obviously shattered by our appearance and there was none of the rancour that I had expected. As he was getting dressed, he was guarded by Don who was somewhat amused by a comment he made to him.

'Where you takin' me then?'

'Walton Lane.'

'That bastard Mulloy had better not be there.'

'Know him do you?'

'Know him! That bastard got me five years. If I ever see him again I'll bloody kill him.'

'Missed your chance then, didn't you?'

'How d'you mean?'

'He was the feller who woke you up by shoving a gun in your face this morning!'

It wasn't Shearer's day. The search recovered some cash that matched the serial numbers of the stolen money, and clothing that forensics later connected to the robbery scene and the stolen car they had escaped in. He later pleaded guilty and was sent to prison.

Don was good to work with, a giant of a man, tough and unrelenting, but loyal and self-motivating. In his massive hands the pickaxe handle he favoured during raids seemed to be no more than a hammer shaft. He was home one night when a neighbour called to say that he had heard sounds coming from the house next door. He was aware that the family were on holiday. Don made his way to the house and discovered that the front door had been forced open. On entering the hallway, he was immediately attacked by two men who came hurtling towards him. He was struck a blow to the head with a heavy silver tray with such force that it completely buckled. Don shook his head to clear his senses and fought back. Within minutes, it was all over. Both men were arrested and required medical treatment themselves.

Eventually they appeared at the Crown Court and pleaded guilty to the burglary and the assault on Don. The judge called him into the witness box to commend him and was obviously impressed by his build. This was shown by what he had to say prior to sentencing the two defendants:

'Had the law not changed some years ago, you may have been facing me charged with a far more serious charge than the assault on Detective Constable Jones. Having seen the stature of the man, it was more like attempted suicide when you attacked him!'

*

I always have had a good memory for faces but names are an entirely different matter. One night I was in the Federal club in Princess Road trying to trace a man who was wanted for robbery. This was a really tough place and it was regularly frequented by criminals. Every time I entered I was aware that there was only one way in and out. I was sitting with Dave Monteith and Alan McFarlane and, at the end of the large bar, was a good-looking dark-haired girl. I knew her face from somewhere but I just couldn't place her. We were there for over an hour and during this time I got the impression she was well aware who we were. It was nagging at me all the time – who the hell was she?

Eventually we left, and as we walked out, she averted her glance from us. Just as we were about to drive away it hit me. I knew she had been circulated as wanted, though it had been a long time ago. We went back inside and, after shooing away the protests of her male companions, we took the woman outside. I checked her bag, found a driving licence and used the car radio to check out the details. I was informed that the licence had been stolen in a robbery some weeks earlier, when a lone woman driver had been attacked in Parliament Street. The victim had been sitting in her car at the traffic lights when thugs had smashed her windscreen and stolen her bag. She had received lacerations to her face and shards of glass in her eyes.

We nicked the girl and took her to the Main Bridewell where she admitted her true identity. She was wanted for wounding another woman, who had lost the sight of an eye after having an ashtray smashed into her face in a fracas in a nightclub in the city. The circulation had been made some eighteen months earlier but somehow her face had stayed in my mind.

She was kept in custody and the following day I was in court at Dale Street over her case. I was most impressed by a young barrister making a bail application for a man accused of housebreaking. He made an ardent plea for the man's freedom, not, he hastened to stress, for his client's benefit but because his grandmother, whom he looked upon as his mother, was dying and needed him in her last hours. The trivial matter of breaking into houses, which his client denied, must not keep him from her deathbed. Having practically reduced the bench to tears, the barrister tried one last ploy. He turned and addressed his client in the dock. 'Tell their Worships in your own words, why do you desire bail today?'

'So I can commit suicide, sir!'

He went down so fast it was as if someone had opened a trap door.

Soon afterwards we were called over to Birkenhead to look into a robbery at a bank in Church Road in Tranmere. Three men had broken into the premises overnight and waited for the staff to arrive in the morning. They had used extreme violence against one employee and escaped with a large quantity of cash. We were told by the divisional officers that there were no leads and that no similar offences had occurred in the vicinity. We did what we could but, frankly, there was nowhere to start the inquiry. Soon afterwards we were called to another case and played no further part in the investigation.

However, sixteen years later one of the robbers walked into Bromborough Police Station and, to the amazed duty constable on the desk, admitted not only this offence but several others in sequence prior to this. Even after all this time, it was affecting his sleep! Despite the passage of time and his contribution, the violence used could not be forgotten and the robbers received six years inside. By chance, I knew a relative of the man who had been attacked and he, too, still suffered from his ordeal. This was a most unusual case in that the attacker and the victim remained affected despite the passage of years.

Sometimes offences took place that beggared belief. In the New Year of 1978 a 34-year-old woman was asleep with her husband in her flat in Toxteth. She was crippled and confined to a wheelchair by day. Two masked knife-wielding men broke through a rear window and confronted the terrified residents. The wife was dragged into her wheelchair and her partner taken to another room. As one intruder ransacked the flat looking for money, the unfortunate women was raped in her wheelchair by his companion.

Her ordeal was not at an end. The men swapped over and she was again viciously raped, still trapped in her wheelchair. After the offenders made good their escape, the couple managed to draw the attention of neighbours to their plight.

This had been a horrific ordeal for the helpless woman and a large-scale inquiry was set in motion to trace her attackers. These were men everyone wanted in custody. I was seconded to assist and, working from

Admiral Street, the net began to widen. We believed that the main intention of the offenders had been theft and the rape was a crime of opportunity. Before the inquiry was completed, however, we were moved to another investigation. We just had to accept the frustration we were more urgently needed elsewhere.

Chapter Thirty-Six

Bomb threats were in the air and, on several occasions, the city centre ground to a halt as the task of searching premises was undertaken. Having performed that role more times than I can remember, I can assure you it is not high on my list of favourite jobs. Always at the back of your mind is the thought – could this be the one?

When an attack did occur, it was at an unlikely scene. Renshaw Street in the heart of the city housed the Department of Employment offices and, as a young bobby, I had often waited for the 82 bus to take me to Speke to pound that beat from the stop just outside. Shortly before midday in early February a firebomb exploded in the toilet area causing extensive damage. Within the hour we had been summoned, along with the Special Branch, to take up the inquiry. What was left of the device was examined and it appeared to be similar to ones already set off in Oxford Street in London in earlier incidents. We braced ourselves for a possible firebomb blitz in the city but it was puzzling why this venue had been chosen. The answer was not long in coming.

Two days later my section assisted in a Special Branch raid on a house in Scarisbrick Drive in the Norris Green area and we discovered a bomb factory.

As well as a revolver and ammunition, a large quantity of explosives were seized, along with detonators and sixteen prepared incendiary devices. The families in the immediate area had to evacuate their homes for several hours, while the explosives were examined by an Army bomb disposal unit. This was a very significant haul. One can only imagine not only the damage these bombs could have caused but also the injuries that may have been sustained.

Inquiries continued through the night and at eight o'clock the next morning a 29-year-old man was arrested as he was about to sit down to his breakfast in a house off Breck Road, near to the city centre. He was interviewed and, eventually, he confessed. He told us he had been visited by two men whose cause he stated he believed in. In general conversation he was asked if he would plant bombs for them and he agreed to do so. The following morning he travelled into the centre, taking with him two of the devices. He intended to plant one at the Army and Navy Stores in Ranleagh Street, just along from the employment offices. He had yet to choose his other target. He may as well have left his name and address at the scene as, incredibly, he signed on at the offices just before going into the toilets to prime the devices. Unfortunately, no one had told him never to set a clock on a bomb by turning it backwards! As he had done so, the device had gone off prematurely as he held it in his hand. It had set his clothing alight and singed his hair. He ran from the scene and disposed of the other device down a grid. Carol was most impressed when my picture and that of Don Jones appeared in the national press showing us searching grids!

The suspect eventually appeared at the Crown Court before Mr Justice Caulfield and pleaded guilty to a variety of charges connected with the incident and the explosives found at his home. Prior to sentence, the judge told him: 'Your arsenal was too large and too comprehensive for you to be considered an amateur. It would have created havoc in this city.'

He sent them down for fourteen years.

The Main Bridewell in Cheapside in the city centre is unique in the history of policing. It is classed as a prison and the Chief Inspector in charge also holds the title of Governor. George Savage was the Governor at this period, as a sergeant he had helped steer me through my probationary days at Lawrence Road. One morning I bumped into Mike while I was booking a prisoner into the Main and George approached us. He asked us if we knew Danny Forrest and we told him that we did – Danny was a nasty piece of work and a regular burglar. He had been remanded in custody and had been due to appear before the court that morning. However, he had noticed a loophole in the security system and had managed to escape from the court complex.

George had reported this to HQ and come to an agreement that if Forrest was arrested in time for his court appearance the matter would not go any further. If he wasn't recaptured then a full-scale inquiry would have to be held. Naturally, George would prefer to do without this. Mike and I readily agreed to hunt for Danny and return him to the cells if we possibly could. Mike had a good contact in the Lodge Lane area who knew Danny and might be able to help us. We drove round there and struck gold right away. She hadn't seen him but she did know the address of this current girlfriend.

'Do you think he will go there?'

'How long has he been on remand?'

'Three weeks – why?'

'What would you want first if you'd just got out, Mr Johnson?'

'A pint or two probably, but I see you point!'

Minutes later we parked up in Holt Road and walked towards the end-terrace house where the girl lived in the ground-floor flat. I was about to go around to the rear when Mike stopped and peered through the gap in the curtains. Putting his hands to his lips, he beckoned me over. I looked into the room and there was Danny, obviously have just enjoyed a moment of significant intimacy. He was lying stark naked, face down on the settee alongside his equally nude girlfriend. My first view of him was his flabby white backside. As I indicated to Mike that I was going round to the rear of the house, he whispered to me:

'I knew that we'd get to the bottom of this!'

Within minutes Danny was back in custody and we returned him to a grateful George back at the Main Bridewell.

The squad enjoyed a good relationship with all of the divisional detectives. We had jointly investigated so many serious crimes with them that a good rapport had been built up. However, there is always one who's prepared to jeopardise such a relationship for his own ends. We'd been called in to help with an armed robbery in the city in which a security man collecting cash from a large store had been confronted by two masked men armed with sawn-off shotguns. He had been clubbed to the ground and the men had escaped on a stolen motorcycle with the cash box. We ran the inquiry along with the local lads for a couple of days. On the second evening, I was on late cover and returned to the station with Dave Monteith just before eleven. I checked the messages that had come into the Robbery Control and saw that there was little of note. I also spoke with a divisional sergeant who assured me that there were no developments that I needed to be aware of.

On my return the following morning I found a hive of activity at the station. Just after dawn the divisional men had executed a search warrant on a house, recovered a shotgun hidden in the outside porch and arrested the 33-year-old occupant. I spoke to the sergeant who, the previous evening, had told me that there were no developments. He was somewhat embarrassed, but in reality it was not his fault. The night before, a man had rung the Robbery Control out of the blue and had given them specific details about the firearm. Someone in the division had decided to withhold this information from the squad members and told the sergeant to obtain a search warrant and arrange that only divisional officers executed it.

I was not too perturbed. It would only take a telephone call to HQ to have us withdrawn and if this officer wanted to play games we had far more important matters to take care of. The division also had a problem, as the man they had in custody was saying nothing to them. Since I had had previous dealings with the prisoner they now wanted me to interview him. I had no difficulty with that – we were all on the same job after all. Dave and I had a chat with him and he told us what the situation was. He refused to name the robbers for fear of reprisals on his family. He was genuinely apprehensive and I could understand why. He did tell us who he had been hiding the gun for but was unable to reveal if these people had committed this particular robbery. From what he let slip, however, we knew these men were active criminals.

He was later charged by divisional officers in regard to this firearm. Within a day or so I arranged for us to be removed from the inquiry. I did not forget it, however. I put my section into looking into the background and associates of the man found with the gun. Dave and Don got the information we required which eventually let to the arrest of the robbers some weeks later. I enjoyed making the telephone call to the division informing them that we had cleared their robbery up.

Chapter Thirty-Seven

Southport, on the northern edges of Merseyside, is a genteel area where many people retire. Prior to the amalgamation of Liverpool Police with parts of Lancashire and Cheshire Police, it had been part of Lancashire Constabulary and even now the general approach to policing was more county than city. The squad had had few dealings with the area but this was to change on the evening of the 28th October 1977.

Marion, a 42-year-old housewife, lived with her businessman husband in a detached house in a leafy secluded cul-de-sac in Formby. She had two daughters, one married, the other single and a member of the Royal Air Force. Marion had been married for twenty-three years and worked part-time in a nearby pharmacy. She was well known in the area and everyone spoke of her with fondness.

This day started like any other. Marion was not due at work and, prior to leaving for his office, her husband brought her a cup of tea in bed. Some time that afternoon he telephoned home and, having finished work, travelled by train from the city centre to Formby. On arrival he was surprised to find the house in darkness as he was expecting Marion to be at home. He entered the house, switched on the hall light and opened the kitchen door to horror.

Marion was slumped in a chair with her head resting on the worktop in a pool of blood. She was heavily bloodstained and her husband tried to revive her. He shouted to neighbours for help and rang for an ambulance, but when medical assistance arrived it was too late – Marion was dead. That night we were called to the scene. There were two immense pools of blood in the kitchen and the walls were extensively spattered and splashed. It was obvious that an attack of great violence had taken place there. The trail of blood continued into the hall and dining room.

Marion had suffered extensive injuries. She had been struck sixteen times with a blunt instrument in a rain of blows that had shattered her skull. Not only that, she had also been stabbed. There were twelve stab wounds in her chest alone, four of them puncturing her heart. It was a heart-breaking way for such a gentle woman to meet her end.

Having set up the Murder Control at Formby station, later that night I returned to the scene with Ken Anderson, who was by now the deputy head of CID. By this time the body had been removed but Ken was appalled by the amount of blood still visible. This had been a frenzied assault which the victim had had no chance of surviving.

The investigation developed gradually. House-to-house inquires were in full swing and I spent the greater part of the next day allocating tasks to the sixty-strong murder team. By now we were aware that Steven, the son-in-law of the deceased, had visited the house on the afternoon of the murder. He had twice been extensively interviewed and he was adamant that Marion had been alive and well when he had left. His movements had been checked and, as a regular visitor to the house, at this stage there no was particular reason to connect him with the murder.

I was reading some statements in the control room when Ken Anderson approached me. He told me he wanted me to re-interview the son-in-law and I decided to take Kevin Cronin in with me. We took Steven to the Chief Superintendent's vacant office and sat him opposite us. He was a slightly-built 23-year-old who seemed quite composed. I was aware that he had been calmly watching TV when his wife had arrived home from her office and had eaten tea with her. There had been nothing out of the ordinary in his behaviour and he had appeared to be quite frank with the first officers he had spoken to. I went over his movements with him for the previous day and he repeated exactly what he had already told the investigators. He had been to a local pub for a couple of drinks and had then gone to his mother-in-law's, leaving at about 3.30 p.m. after a chat and a cup of tea. However, I had the feeling he was not telling us the truth. Even if his demeanour seemed composed, there was something in his eyes that told me he was our man. I glanced over at Kevin and he gave me a small nod of the head. We were a good interviewing team. We knew from experience which way each would take the questioning. Something told me that this was a vital interview.

'What did you and Marion talk about?' I asked him.

'I don't remember.'

We carried on for some minutes discussing his visit and he now became cagey and suspicious.

He was asked when he had last called at the house by chance and he made no reply. He stared at the floor for several moments and I put it to him again. Had Marion known he was going to call? Once more we could get no response. Eventually, after more silence, he spoke.

'I just called there. I wish I hadn't.'

'Why?'

'You know.'

'We don't know.'

'I wouldn't be here if I hadn't called.'

Again we went over his movements after he had left the house and who he had seen. He repeated the details of his journey home and I told him that we had a witness who had seen him on the train and said he appeared different. He refused to discuss this.

'You appreciate we're involved in a murder investigation?'

'Yes, I know.'

'Do you know anything about how Marion met her death?'

'No, she was all right when I left her.'

'How did you get on with her?'

'All right. I get on all right with her.'

'Did anyone call at the house while you were there?'

'No, no one.'

Once more we went over his movements during his visit, again he repeated exactly what he had already said.

'What did you talk about?'

'We just talked.'

'What about?'

'I don't remember.'

'It's strange you not being able to remember. Where were you when you were talking to her?'

'It wasn't in the kitchen.'

'I didn't say it was.'

'Well, it wasn't in the kitchen.'

'Where did it take place?'

He made no reply.

'Can you remember any of the conversation?'

'No, nothing at all.'

'I feel it's a little strange that your memory of yesterday afternoon is so vague, considering the event that has occurred is so out of the ordinary.'

He made no reply but then stayed silent for moments, staring at the floor. Suddenly he straightened up and looked me in the eye.

'I didn't do it, she was all right when I left.'

'Why have you been silent?'

'I've been thinking.'

'You look like you've got something on your mind.'

He made no reply and, after a short while, he repeated what he had maintained had taken place during the visit.

'Where did you talk?'

'I don't remember.'

'Was it in the kitchen?'

'No, it wasn't in there.'

This desire to have us believe he had not entered the kitchen was making the hairs on the back of my neck stand up.

'Was it in the sitting room?'

No reply.

'Was in the dining room?'

No reply.

'It's strange that you can't remember or don't wish to say where this conversation took place.'

He made no answer.

'Do you call to see your mother-in-law often?'

'Now and again.'

'Why?'

'I go with my wife.'

I asked him if he often called to see her on his own and he refused to answer. Again he appeared to draw on some inner strength and made a request.

'Can I have a cup of tea, please?'

Kevin did the honours and we sat in silence, sipping tea in the most bizarre circumstances.

When we resumed the interview, we again chatted about his previous dealings with Marion but, like a dog with a bone, I soon brought the discussion back to what I was knew he was reluctant to talk about.

'Do you remember anything about the conversation?'

'No.'

'Do you remember where you talked?'

'No.'

'It's important for you to try and remember everything you can about this visit.'

'Why?'

'If you're correct, you're the last person to see her alive.'

'So what?'

'If she mentioned anything at all, no mater how trivial, it may be of vital importance to us.'

'I don't understand.'

'What we mean is, she may have said she was expecting another caller.'

He got up and walked to the window, staring out over Lord Street.

'I didn't do it.'

He stood there motionless for several moments, saying nothing. Abruptly he returned to his chair and sat down.

'She was alive when I left her.'

I went over the facts with him as he again said that he had called at the house by chance and could remember nothing of the conversation or where it had taken place.

'However, you do know where it didn't take place.'

'In the kitchen.'

'Why are you so sure of that?'

'I just am.'

'Don't you think that strange?'

'How do you mean?'

'That your memory is so vague about the whole afternoon.'

'She was all right when I left her.'

I decided to move the conversation away for a moment and we discussed his own background and, as we were comparative strangers to the area, the geography of the locality. In response to some mundane question he retorted: 'She was all right when I left.'

He stared at the floor again for several long minutes and repeated himself. 'She was all right when I left.'

'Why are you doing that?'

'Doing what?'

'Staring at the floor.'

'Because of what you asked me.'

'I was only asking about the area.'

'No, not that, about her.'

'You mean Marion?'

'Yes.'

'Are you upset about me asking you?'

'No, but she was all right when I left.'

He then began another session of staring at the floor. After several minutes I asked him what the matter was.

'I went to the house for a cup of tea and a chat.'

'Why are you behaving like this?'

'Like what?'

'You keep staring at the floor and out of the window.'

'I just am.'

'Why are you doing it?'

'You think I did it, don't you?'

'Do I?'

'You both think I killed her. You know you do.'

'Did you kill her?'

As first he did not reply but again stared at the floor. 'She was all right when I left her.'

'Are you sure you did her no harm?'

'I can't tell you.'

'Have you done something you can't bring yourself to talk about?'

'What?'

'Look, you repeat endlessly that she was all right but can give no further details. Even in your own version you're very vague.'

'Just because I can't remember, doesn't mean I did it.'

'What do you mean by "did it"?'

'She was all right when I left, you can't prove anything different.'

'Why should we wish to prove any different?'

'Well, she was.'

'I'm not satisfied with your explanation. I feel that you're definitely hiding something.'

'You two think I did it.'

Now was the time to take the crucial step. It could drive him further into his inner self or reveal the truth. It was a gamble I had to take. I spoke very quietly.

'You did kill her, didn't you?'

'I was fixing my keyring when it happened.'

'When what happened?'

The answer was simplicity in itself.

'I killed her. I was fixing my keyring and I went in the garage for a hammer. I came back in and she called me for my tea. She was nagging at me about not being good enough for her daughter and not wanting work. I lost my temper and hit her with the hammer.'

I took a very deep breath to calm myself down. It was all over.

'What happened next?'

'I don't really remember. I put the hammer back in the garage. It was on a worktop by the side door, then I left.'

'She had also been stabbed.'

'I don't remember doing that to her.'

He went on to explain that he was fixing his keyring with the hammer, although he failed to convince me that he needed such an implement to carry out the repair.

'Do you wish to make a written statement?'

'Yes, I will.'

He asked me to write the statement in which he confirmed that he had visited the house that afternoon. As they talked in the kitchen Marion had been ironing. According to him, she had been remonstrating with him about his lack of work. He alleged that he had wanted to fix his key chain and had gone into the garage to get a hammer. When he returned with it, she continued to nag him. His temper blew up and he remembered hitting her on the head a few times with the hammer, which he described as being two pounds in weight.

He recalled there was blood all over the kitchen, the rest was a blur until he got a grip of himself. He described where he had replaced the hammer in the garage, then had got the train home. He concluded that he was sorry this terrible thing had happened. He had not even been drunk. It was just his temper getting the better of him.

He signed this statement which both Kevin and I endorsed as witnesses. I again cautioned him and told him that I was arresting him for the murder. He simply replied, 'OK.'

We placed him back in the cells, then made our way to the control room to inform an exultant Ken.

Frank Carthy recovered the hammer from the garage and forensic examination at the house revealed a knife – an ornamental stiletto hanging on the wall in the lounge. This was found to have traces of blood on it but, most significantly, a minute part of the tip was missing. I was present when a further examination of the deceased was

287

carried out by a consultant radiologist. The X-ray revealed that the tip was lodged in the dead woman's ribs and it was later recovered. Later that night I formally charged Steven with Marion's murder.

Months later he appeared in the famous No. 1 court at Liverpool Crown Court at St George's Hall before Mr Justice Caulfield. Mr Ward, QC, appeared for the Crown and Mr Wright, QC, defended. Steven admitted the killing but denied murder. I was called to give evidence and, having done so, I was only cross-examined on minor points. The statement that I had obtained went unchallenged.

The defence sought a manslaughter verdict on the grounds of diminished responsibility and provocation. The court was told that Steven had been involved in a car smash some months earlier which had left him unconscious for five days. In his evidence on his own behalf, he told the jury that, since that accident, he had been forced to leave his job and had not worked since.

On the day of the killing he had visited Marion after a lunchtime drink at a nearby pub. She had been going on at him about his unemployment and he was under the impression that his temper had got the better of him. As far has he could remember, he hit her over the head with a hammer but had no recollection of the knife wounds.

After hearing all the evidence the jury retired and, after five hours of deliberation, they rejected his plea and returned a unanimous verdict: guilty of murder. He was then sentenced to life imprisonment by Mr Justice Caulfield who told him that he must face the penalty laid down by law for murder. He stood composed as sentence was passed but his mother collapsed and had to be helped from the court by relatives who comforted the sobbing woman.

Once again, two families had been destroyed by a senseless killing. No one could gain any satisfaction from the case but I was content with the part that I had played in its detection. Kevin and I had brought the murderer to justice because of our interview. We had handled him in just the right manner and he had eventually been able to face the terrible truth.

Steven's conviction was to be my last murder investigation for several years. The hierarchy of the service was changing. The likes of Tom Whittlestone and Gordon McKenzie had retired. They were bosses I had been prepared to work myself into the ground for, thorough professionals and fiercely protective of their men.

I was now to be posted back to uniform duties on the Wirral. Fourteen years had passed since I had last worn the blue serge and in that time I had gained enormous experience of the investigation of serious organised crime and murder. Unfortunately, this would be of little use in my new role. I had been summoned to HQ and brusquely given the news by an assistant chief constable that I was now considered expendable. It seemed that my style of 'in your face' policing was no longer wanted. I recalled the words of Morris, the armed robber who had warned me that certain people wanted me out of the way. Unfortunately the knife came from the direction I was least expecting.

I returned to the Serious Crime Squad suite at Walton Lane to find a deserted office. As I cleared out my desk and began to dispose of old files, memories flooded back. Shortly afterwards, Lawrence Road closed for the last time as an operational station. It was traditional that officers who had worked at any of the old stations would be invited to say farewell at a function to mark the station's passage into history. My invitation never arrived. I can only presume that, having been posted to the far side of the Mersey, I had been overlooked. I was not to have the opportunity to say goodbye to the old girl.

Most of my career had been spent as a detective. It was more than just a job, it was my way of life. Although I am not proud of it, I had to accept the fact that work often came first in my list of priorities. There are some debts I can never repay to Carol. However, my life as a detective was now behind me and I had to accept the reality. At least Birkenhead was the busiest nick in the force area, so I would not get too bored.

Carol and I went for a meal that night and we talked about the changes we could expect in my new posting. The advantages, when looked at in perspective, certainly outweighed the disadvantages. It was closer to home and I could confidently expect to work far fewer hours. Only a handful of the officers I had started with remained in the squad and more than one had had his health ruined by the stress and horror of the inquiries. Others were shortly to be posted back to uniform as the new brooms swept clean.

As Carol pointed out, one advantage of working a uniformed three-shift system was that she would always know what time I was coming home.

She should have known better.

Epilogue

These incidents were not to be the last murders and deaths that I was to encounter in the years to come. One of these was the death of 21-year-old Diane Sindall, a lovely girl from a close-knit family. Her body was found in an alleyway off Borough Road in Birkenhead just after noon on Saturday, 2nd August 1986. The investigation leading to the eventual conviction of her killer is outlined in my book about those times, *Chasing the Dragons*. Diane is the only murder victim on Merseyside to have a permanent memorial erected on the spot where she met her end. The inscription reads:

> *Diane Sindall*
> *Murdered 2.8.1986*
> *Because she was a woman*
> *In memory of all our sisters*
> *who have been raped and murdered*
> *We will never let it be forgotten*

Her death had one common factor with all of those that I had been involved in over the years.

> *I will never forget any of you.*

Closure

During the early evening of 23rd April 1996 the *Liverpool Echo* was delivered to my home. By now retired from the service, I picked it up and casually glanced at the front page. Startled by what I was reading, the words leapt out at me.

MANHUNT!
CHILD KILLER ON THE LOOSE AFTER LEAP TO FREEDOM

Beneath the banner headline a face I would never forget stared out at me. Ernie, little Margaret's killer, had escaped from custody. The article revealed that he had been allowed to visit Liverpool under the supervision of a prison officer and, at his sister's house in Wavertree, he escaped through a toilet window. A massive search was now in progress for him. The whole background of the case was reported with comments from residents and neighbours who remembered only too well the dreadful event that had occurred in their midst over two decades earlier.

I made my way to my study and, after a brief search, retrieved the file which I was seeking. I scanned the contents and made several notes, after which I telephoned the police office where the hunt was being co-ordinated. Having given an officer details that might assist in their inquiries for Ernie, I made a coffee and sat with one of my cats, Smudge, purring on my knee. As I read through the file, memories came back as if from yesterday.

Over the years I had thought of the case from time to time. It had crossed my mind several times that under normal circumstances Margaret would in all probability have been a mother herself by now. I had had no idea that Ernie was still serving his sentence. I had presumed that he would have long been released. Now twenty-one years later he was back in my life. I had told the investigator that he had close connections in the Netherley district of Liverpool. Only hours later, he was sighted in that area by uniformed officers. After a long chase he was eventually caught and returned to the cells.

APPENDIX

Detective Chief Inspector Mike Mulloy
COMMENDATIONS AND AWARDS

1964

18th June   Chief Constable's commendation for outstanding work in the detection of crime.

18th June   Chief Constable's commendation for excellent work in the detection of crime.

1965

28th August   Chief Constable's commendation for excellent work in the detection of crime.

28th August   Chief Constable's commendation for an outstanding record of crime arrests while a member of the Commando Squad.

1967
26th July   Chief Constable's commendation
                       for outstanding work in the
                       detection of crime.

1969
24th November   Chief Constable's commendation
                       for outstanding work in the
                       detection of crime.

1971
30th March   Chief Constable's commendation
                       for an outstanding record of arrests
                       in the detection of serious crime.

1972
22nd May   Chief Constable's commendation
                       for outstanding work in the
                       detection of serious crime as a
                       member of the Special Section.

6th September   Granted the Liverpool and Bootle
                       Police Authority Award of Merit for
                       his dedication, ability, inspiration
                       and devotion to duty displayed in
                       the detection of serious crime. The
                       citation included the arrest of a male
                       who had committed over 300
                       robberies and two gangs who were
                       responsible for numerous armed
                       robbery, burglary and wounding
                       offences.

1974

5th August   Judge's commendation by the Recorder of Liverpool, His Honour Mr Justice Lyons, for intelligent work and determination displayed during a six-month inquiry leading to the arrest and conviction of a gang responsible for burglary offences throughout the North West region. He was also commended by the Detective Chief Superintendent.

4th December   Chief Constable's commendation for excellent work in the detection of serious crime and the successful investigation of a number of armed robberies while a member of the Regional Crime Squad.

1975

11th March   Chief Constable's commendation for outstanding leadership of special Robbery Squad in Toxteth.

3rd December   Chief Constable's commendation for excellent work in the case of the murder of a seven-year-old girl.

1976

11th July   Judge's commendation by His Honour Mr Justice Lawton for work in a complicated conspiracy and theft inquiry and the eventual arrest of thirty-six offenders.

1977

15th February   Detective Chief Superintendent's commendation for outstanding work in the investigation of several armed robberies and the arrest of the offenders.

1978

25th January   Chief Constable's commendation for outstanding performance in the field of crime detection while a member of the Serious Crime Squad and, in particular, for excellent work in cases of armed robbery and murder.

1979

26th June   Judge's commendation by His Honour Mr Justice Price for initiative leading to arrests and the recovery of stolen property in a case of burglary.

25th July   Chief Superintendent's commendation for interest, determination and attention to duty leading to the convictions of offenders for burglary and receiving.

10th October   Commended by the Wirral Justices for utmost efficiency and courage in a case of serious public disorder during which he and a number of police officers were injured.

1980
8th February   Chief Superintendent's
                        commendation for excellent work
                        resulting in a number of arrests for
                        crime.

1981
9th December   Chief Superintendent's
                        commendation for the efficient,
                        patient and entirely professional way
                        an injured and mentally disturbed
                        young woman who was armed and
                        showing violent suicidal tendencies
                        was dealt with.

1982
4th January   Certificate of Merit awarded by the
                        Royal Society for the Prevention of
                        Cruelty to Animals in recognition of
                        his performance during the rescue of
                        an Alsatian dog from an attic in a
                        derelict house under extremely
                        hazardous conditions.
16th December   Commendation from the Liverpool
                        and Shipwreck and Humane Society
                        for his courageous actions which
                        resulted in the successful rescue of
                        several persons trapped in a car
                        which was in danger of exploding.

1983

27th April	Chief Superintendent's commendation for intelligent and most professional policing during an exercise which resulted in the arrest of a determined escapee from prison.
26th July	Judge's commendation by His Honour Mr Justice Lawton, for conduct throughout the entire case of perjury and attempt to pervert the course of justice which prevented a miscarriage of justice.
17th August	Chief Superintendent's commendation for skill and initiative in a complicated serious criminal inquiry leading to the detection and conviction of the offender.
8th September	Chief Constable's commendation for courage, skill and determination in disarming an emotionally unstable woman in possession of a carving knife who was holding two social workers against their will with the weapon.

1984

27th January   Awarded HM The Queen's Long
Service and Good Conduct Medal.

1st February   Chief Superintendent's
commendation for excellent team-
work, initiative and professionalism
resulting in an impressive number of
arrests for crime.

27th July   Chief Superintendent's
commendation for excellent work
resulting in numerous arrests for
serious crime.

1986

1st March   Chief Superintendent's
commendation for outstanding
leadership of the Wirral Crime
Squad.

9th April   Chief Constable's commendation
for professionalism and application
to duty resulting in the recovery of a
large amount of drugs for
importation and the arrest and
conviction of determined criminals
who were sentenced to long terms of
imprisonment. A letter of
appreciation was also received from
Her Majesty's Customs and Excise
in respect of this inquiry.

1987

17th March
Judge's commendation by the Recorder of Liverpool, His Honour Mr Justice Temple, regarding an investigation into a serious case of armed robbery.

12th November
Chief Superintendent's commendation for good work in a serious case of indecency involving young boys.

1988

24th February
Judge's commendation by His Honour Mr Justice Naylor for the painstaking investigations leading to a number of arrests in a serious case of drug trafficking in 'Operation Chepstow'.

19th May
Chief Constable's commendation for professionalism in an inquiry into drug-related crimes leading to the arrest of prolific criminal individuals. He was also commended by His Honour Mr Justice Taylor at Liverpool Crown Court.

8th August
Judge's commendation by His Honour Mr Justice Nance for the tremendous amount of work entailed in a serious and complicated drug trafficking case in 'Operation Brynmoss'.

1989

20th January Judge's commendation by His Honour Mr Justice Arthur for patient, skilful and accomplished work in a major drugs conspiracy namely 'Operation Bedford'.

27th October Judge's commendation by His Honour Mr Justice Lachs for drive and determination displayed leading to the successful prosecution of a determined gang of drug suppliers during 'Operation Steeple'.

1991

9th May Chief Constable's commendation for investigative skills, professionalism and determination during a major operation which led to the arrest of many offenders of an organised and professional ring for serious offences of supply of hard drugs.

9th May Chief Constable's commendation for determination, initiative and dedication to duty displayed while conducting complex inquiries into numerous drug dealings known operationally as 'Dial-a-Smack', which resulted in the conviction of a team of highly organised criminals.

9th May Chief Constable's commendation for devotion to duty, good observations and interrogative skills displayed during an operation which led to the arrest of many offenders who dealt in hard drugs to the value of over £500,000, who were sentenced to long terms of imprisonment.

9th May Chief Constable's commendation for leadership, surveillance and professionalism displayed during an operation which became the largest drug investigation on Merseyside leading to the closure of a drugs network and the successful conviction of its members.

9th May Chief Constable's commendation for professionalism, skill and dedication to duty displayed during an investigation into major suppliers and dealers of controlled drugs which resulted in the conviction of one of Merseyside's most violent and prolific criminals.

Also available in Arrow

THE GOOD GUYS WEAR BLACK

Steve Collins

SO19, the Metropolitan Police Special Firearms Wing is an awesome squad of gunfighters who daily defend the public from evil. Here Sergeant Steve Collins, who led Black Team, the hardest and most renowned team within the unit, tells their story. Yardies, international drug barons, IRA enforcers and celebrity South London gangsters and hitmen have all been taken off the streets by the true-life heroes of SO19 either in handcuffs or in bodybags. The tensions and camaraderie of a team who daily risk death has never been captured so vividly on the page.

'Gripping, action-packed . . . compelling' *Sun*

KILLING FOR COMPANY

Brian Masters

On February 9th 1983 Dennis Nilsen was arrested at his Muswell Hill home, after human remains had been identified as the cause of blocked drains. Within days he had confessed to fifteen gruesome murders over a period of four years. His victims, all young homosexual men, had never been missed. Brian Masters, with Nilsen's full cooperation, has produced a study of a murderer's mind which is unique of its kind.

'Probably the best thing of its kind since *In Cold Blood* . . . a classic study in criminal mentality'
Colin Wilson, *Yorkshire Post*

'*Killing For Company* must stand as one of the most remarkable and accurate accounts ever written of the singular relationship between a mass murderer and a society. Brian Masters, in the writing, has achieved the impossible. Though dealing with sensational and horrific matters he has managed, God knows how, to treat his material with such objectivity and restraint that what we have is not a penny dreadful from the Hammer House of Horror, but a bloody masterpiece.' Beryl Bainbridge, *Observer*

'A truly awesome tale, brilliantly told' *Literary Review*

Also available in Arrow

MINDLESS MURDERS

John Dunning

A murder without motive is the most chilling crime of all. And the twenty seemingly pointless murders described here are all the more horrifying because every one is true. The dissected body found still partly deep-frozen in the park, the corpse cooked through in the sauna, the murder of an elderly woman from Black Mamba venom – these are just some of the extraordinary cases described in *Mindless Murders*.

'John Dunning has the journalist's eye for the gruesome, for human oddity, and for sheer dramatic tension' Colin Wilson

STRANGE DEATHS

John Dunning

Fifteen true stories of the most shocking and unusual murders of the twentieth century, each one retold in frighteningly accurate detail by an outstanding historian of crime. Stories that are guaranteed to send shivers of terror down your spine.

'John Dunning has the journalist's eye for the gruesome, for human oddity, and for sheer dramatic tension' Colin Wilson

Also available in Arrow

HELTER SKELTER

Vincent Bugliosi with Curt Gentry

The true story behind one of the most infamous mass murder cases ever.

On August 9th 1969, seven people were found shot, stabbed and bludgeoned to death in Los Angeles. America watched in fascinated horror as the killers were tried and convicted. But the real questions went unanswered. How did Charles Manson make his 'family' kill for him? What made these young men and women kill again and again with no trace of remorse? Did the murders continue even after Manson's imprisonment?

No matter how much you think you know about this case, this book will shock you.

Including a chilling, 64-page photographic record of the victims, the killers, the evidence

'The fullest story of the Manson case anybody ever is likely to get' *Wall Street Journal*

'A valuable book on a lurid subject . . . A record of savagery and official bungling' *Time*

'Continuously fascinating . . . Bugliosi does not disappoint' *New York Magazine*

MY DARK PLACES

James Ellroy

On the evening of 21 June 1958 Geneva Hilliker Ellroy left her home in El Monte, California. She was found strangled the next day. Her 10-year-old son James was confronted with the news of the killing on his return from a weekend away with his father.

Jean's murderer was never found, but her death had an enduring legacy on her son who spent his early adult years as a petty criminal. Only in 1994, following the publication of a series of critically acclaimed novels, was James Ellroy ready to confront his past. He returned to LA, and with the help of veteran detective Bill Stoner, reopened the casebook of the 38-year-old-killing. Unflinchingly and systematically he confronted every detail, every clue and each shocking revelation.

The result is one of the few classics of crime non-fiction and autobiography to appear in the last few decades; a hypnotic trip to America's underbelly and one man's tortured soul.

'The outstanding American crime writer of his generation' *Independent*

'The most distinctive crime writer of his generation' *John Williams, Sunday Times*

'A gripping and quite awesome form of literature' Tom Hiney, *Express*

'A *tour de force* of confessional writing' *TLS*

'Ellroy proves that he is more than just a crime writer, he is one of the best and most important writers in America today' *Vox*